Praise for *A Taste o*

CW00546728

"This is a captivating read for anyone who cares about the food
and especially those with an interest in a career in food. I can tell you
from having sampled Renee Guilbault's amazing cooking that she knows
how to combine incredibly delicious taste with health and sustainability
and that's what this book brings out—a truly delicious 'recipe' for what's
achievable in the industry."

ERIK FYRWALD, CEO, Syngenta Group

"Reading this book gave me so many a-ha moments—I wish I had
received advice like this when I was starting out as a young manager. I
want everyone on my team to read it, no matter where they are on their
career journey!"

MAISIE GANZLER, chief strategy and brand officer, Bon Appétit
Management Company

"Renee Guilbault reached the pinnacle of the food industry and now
opens the door so that anyone with talent and motivation can follow in
her footsteps. This is the definitive insider's guide to the food industry.
I wish I had this book when I was starting my journey into the world
of food."

SAM POLK, CEO, Everytable

"Renee Guilbault shares her career journey in a direct, humorous, and
authentic way. Filled with insights and advice (and delicious recipes!),
this book is a much-needed resource for anyone interested in, or navigating their way through, a career in the food industry."

CATHERINE LEDERER, SVP, Food & Beverage, Founder's Table Restaurant
Group (Chopt Salad and Dos Toros)

"A must-read book for anyone looking to examine a career path and
take the food industry by storm!. Engaging, practical, and applicable—
well done!"

SYLVIA BANDERAS COFFINET, GM Multicultural Brand Partnerships
& Marketing, Vox Media

"Renee Guilbault's searingly candid, deliciously relatable, and invaluably instructive insider's guide delivers the goods. This is a game-changing read for anyone who wants to build a thriving and meaningful career in the industry."

CASEY GLEASON, VP, Food, sweetgreen

"Who better to guide you through the twists and turns of a career in food than a professional who has lived it and seen all sides? Renee Guilbault captures her entertaining journey from server to leader with characteristic honesty and humor. Here is your opportunity to learn from the best."

SEBASTIAN WRIGHT, New Formats Leader, Amazon

"Renee Guilbault breaks it down and tells it like it is, brutally honest and holds nothing back. *A Taste of Opportunity* is Renee's playbook for career success. Anyone looking to make it in the food industry would be foolish to pass up on this treasure trove of insider secrets."

IRFAN DAMA, Indian Chef Consultant

"The opportunities are limitless for those willing to show up, be honest, honor their agreements, and work—and this book is a wonderful reminder of how to excel in the food-service industry and achieve the proverbial American Dream, regardless of education or background."

JILL OVERDORF, vice-chair, Los Angeles Food Policy Council; founder, The Produce Ambassador

"*A Taste of Opportunity* is a career guide that reads like a delicious full-course meal. It is filled with inspirational stories, useful tips and clear guidance for those who want to not only make a career in the food industry but make meaning and impact."

PAMELA SLIM, award-winning author, *Body of Work* and *The Widest Net*

A TASTE OF OPPORTUNITY

An Insider's Guide to Boosting Your Career, Making Your Mark, & Changing the Food Industry from Within

A TASTE OF
OPPORTUNITY

RENEE GUILBAULT

● ● PAGE TWO

Cataloging in publication information is available from Library and Archives Canada.
ISBN 978-1-77458-247-3 (paperback)
ISBN 978-1-77458-248-0 (ebook)
ISBN 978-1-77458-311-1 (audiobook)

Page Two
pagetwo.com

Edited by Melissa Edwards
Copyedited by Steph VanderMeulen
Proofread by Melissa Kawaguchi
Cover and interior design by Taysia Louie

essayerfoodconsulting.com

For every person who has ever wanted more for their life and didn't know how to make it happen.

CONTENTS

RECIPES IN THIS BOOK

FOREWORD
A GATEWAY TO THE WORLD

WE ALL COME to the food world in our own unique ways. As for me, I just knew it. Right from my teenage years in Holland, I just knew that the hospitality industry was going to be my destiny. Don't ask me why. Nobody in my family had worked in it, and I had not been that exposed to restaurants, hotels, or cafés in my daily life. I just loved the idea of working in that world—and especially the idea of being able to work truly anywhere.

Throughout my high school years, I got the most wonderful taste of this industry and gained hands-on work experience in restaurants, bars, hotels, and coffee shops. I absolutely loved it, and those experiences just reconfirmed my belief in my desired destination. Four years at the Hotel Management School Maastricht in the Netherlands solidified that foundation and successfully seeded my future. I was ready for takeoff.

A couple of years later, I found myself as an assistant café manager at the Westin Peachtree Plaza hotel in Atlanta, Georgia—a place that became my launching platform for seventeen amazing years at Starwood Hotels and Resorts. The Atlanta hospitality industry welcomed me with open arms, just as it has and continues to do for so many others. I got the chance to learn, grow, lead, and move around to different locations, all while working with and serving some of the most interesting people from all over the world. Years later, leading Food & Beverage for Starwood in Europe, the Middle East, and Africa, my life changed again when a recruiter tapped me on the shoulder and posed a question that opened a new and surprising opportunity: Would I be interested in having a conversation about leading an innovative food program with a worldwide impact that would nourish and inspire employees across the world? As it turns out, all of those varied years of experiences across the global hospitality industry had made me a solid candidate for this unique, high-impact role.

The rest is history. I joined Google in 2012 to lead their famous Food at Work program, and took on the company's vision to offer delightful, sustainable, and healthy food experiences—a program that has since grown to serve more than 225,000 people worldwide a day, with more than sixty million meals served annually. I helped build an international ecosystem, and in my present role as VP of Global Workplace Programs, I now have the opportunity (and responsibility) to use that same ecosystem to contribute to making the world better and more sustainable—one step at a time.

I could not imagine all of the meaning, rewards, and opportunity that would present themselves to me when I first started working in coffee shops as a young teenager. It wasn't always easy, and there were moments that were more difficult than I can express—just as there will be in your own career. But it is my most fervent belief that, for each of us, every one of our experiences—even the ones that are so, so hard—help us grow. That pain is not for nothing. It's what helps us become *better*.

That's why this book is so important. I worked with Renee at Google as she oversaw several areas of business across our North and South American operations (including our Mountain View HQ) as a leader for one of the valued vendor partners who bring our extraordinary workplace programs to life every day. I know that her own story—all of her direct experience with nearly every facet of the food world, and with all of its highs and lows—is living proof of the type of impact that any individual from any background can have on our world when they commit themselves to moving forward in this industry and following their passions. She has walked through the fire—both its joyful warmth and its stinging burn—and now, like me, she is in a position to make change and to put her values into action on a massive scale. And if you want it enough, you can carry yourself into that position, too.

Renee's journey is unique to her, as mine was to me, and as yours will be to you. But, as she says in this book, "it's up to you to decide how big and bold you want to go." If you can envision success for yourself, and if you can imagine an industry that is better because you chose to actively play your own part in making it that way, then I know your journey can be magical. All you need to do is bring your full self to the table, every day.

Take it from me. Never in my wildest dreams could I have imagined that my first management job with a team of eight all those years ago could lead me to such an extraordinary opportunity to have not only a positive impact on my team of employees and vendor partners (now 13,000!), but also the privilege of working to solve some of the largest health, nutrition, and sustainability issues of our generation in the process. And all this supported by an organization that deeply values innovation and striving for "moonshot-level outcomes" with every single thing we do. From a team of eight individuals to a team of 13,000 team members and partner organizations, all working together to serve 325,000 meals a day and growing by the second. The opportunity is real.

But don't take just my word for it. Dig into this book. Learn what is waiting out there for you. Get inspired, find your passion, and, most importantly, get going. You won't regret it.

MICHIEL BAKKER

Vice President, Global Workplace Programs, Google

Don't forget to check this out! You do NOT want to miss these insights.

INTRODUCTION
A STANDING INVITATION TO
THE CAREER OF YOUR DREAMS

LET ME START by saying it like it really is. Everything is possible for you in this industry. *Everything.* You can make a ton of money. You can have the life of creativity and freedom you want. You can make an impact on the lives of others. You can travel the world. You can even *change* the world.

Food is a trillion-dollar industry in America, and it's growing by the second. It touches every part of our lives and can be found anywhere we go—and most of the people who work in this industry aren't the famous chefs with sharp knives and sharper tongues you see on TV. They're everyday people like you and me, working in all kinds of different roles and sectors, far beyond the restaurants where many got their start. If you love anything about food—growing it, shopping for it, preparing it, serving it, dreaming about it, reading about it, talking about it, eating it—you can find a way to have a soulful, satisfying, and even lucrative long-term career.

And what's truly and uniquely amazing about the industry—despite the obvious deliciousness factor—is that there is only one requirement for entry. *You.* You and your own personal commitment to showing up and learning new skills. What other jobs you've had, how old you are, or even how far you went in school are not important. The food world is a place where formal education doesn't matter nearly as much as how you show up to do your job every day. *Grit required. College degree or a personal connection to the C-suite? Not so much.*

Take it from me—I am a high school dropout, and I have worked in the food industry in one form or another since I was seventeen years old. Family circumstances led me to leave school and make it out in the world on my own, so the eleventh grade is as far as I got in terms of traditional education. Did that hold me back in this industry? Not one bit. The food world provided me with an incredible array of opportunities despite my lack of that diploma.

Over the years, I have learned that the keys to a successful career in this industry are your resilience, talent, discipline, hospitality, warmth, ability to follow directions, and just simply being a person who is easy to work with and who keeps their promises. If you can bring these qualities to the table, then you have everything you need to achieve incredible success, earn a solid income, and even contribute to some of the most important societal and environmental issues of our time.

This book is designed to help anyone who wants a career in food, whether you're just starting out as an hourly worker, ready to move into management, or looking ahead to executive leadership and wondering how to create positive change in the industry. I'm going to share with you all my experiences—from soup to nuts (*and you're also going to find out how much I adore cheesy food puns*)—and give you a real-life look at the hard knocks, failures, humiliations, and successes you can expect at every stage as you discover for yourself the power of what's possible in this business. You'll get a peek into my perspective as a veteran food world executive, a behind-the-scenes insider, a chef, a dreamer, a consumer, an industry advocate, and even a mom. Sometimes I'll wear the hat of a critic as I dig into some of the things that are deeply wrong in the food world, and I'll invite you to become a part of the change that truly needs to come. I want you to see this industry the way I do—as a career home where everything you can imagine is within reach—and I want to help you fall in love with it the same way I did. More than that, I want to see you *rise*.

To support you on your journey, at the end of each chapter I'm going to equip you with "the mise you need to succeed," also known as getting into Mise Mode. This is a career-development version of "mise en place" (pronounced *meez-on-ploss*), the standard chef's organizational process for making sure every ingredient and tool they need is prepped, organized, and in one place before they even start cooking. As any chef will tell you, if you want to successfully cook, plate, and serve the most complex, high-touch menus imaginable, you need a well-prepared mise en place. Otherwise, you're better off sticking to the lemonade stand on your front lawn. So consider each Mise section like a little career workstation: "Mindset Shift" will show you a new way to think about your relationship to your work, "Trade Secret" will arm you with the best tips and tricks for getting through the tough parts, and the "Leadership Lowdown" will help you keep your eyes on the prize through every stage of your career. As a bonus, each Mise Mode workstation will also feature a scannable link to your "Insider Dish"—a special video interview with a notable food-industry professional who will share their own personal experiences in navigating this exciting, challenging, one-of-a-kind, and *always* flavorful way of life.

You're also going to get some recipes along the way because this is a book about making a career in *food*, people! I want you to taste what I taste, to feel the layers of meaning in food, and to see all the ways it shows up to enhance your life. You know, kind of like a scrumptious and addictive "storytelling" lasagne. Put together with the full list you'll find in the digital cookbook (which includes pretty much every dish mentioned in this book—including the just-mentioned "Storytelling" Lasagne—and which you can find directions to on page 235), these recipes are some of my most foolproof and celebrated dishes—*she says with hands on hips*—but more importantly, they are also windows into my edible soul and will capture the moments you are about to read about in a way words never can.

Now, grab some popcorn (I like mine sprinkled with an obscene amount of Tajín) and settle in, because I'm going to show you how to make all of it possible—and it's a ride that's going to require some snacks! This book is a journey, an invitation, and a love letter, too. The world of food is beautiful and significant, and if you commit to staying in it and succeeding at it, it will change your life in the best possible ways, just as it changed mine. I can't wait to show it to you.

Part One

GETTING STARTED IN THE WORLD OF FOOD

1

WHAT'S ON THE MENU

Four Kick-Ass Reasons to Build a Life in Food

When you aren't satisfied with what you have, you move forward, **and you do something about it.**

THERE ARE SO MANY PATHS to success in the food world—and not just success, but also fulfillment, joy, passion, and *meaning*. Getting to the top is not just about serving up a three-star Michelin meal at a fancy-schmancy restaurant. And the rewards that come from starting at "the bottom" go so far beyond dishing out those paper folders of greasy yet undeniably exquisite french fries from some fast-food joint. This industry is huge, and it's complex, and it's evolving; it has a place for everything you might be capable of, and it's integrated into every facet of every life on this planet. I mean, just think about it: food is the most powerful commodity in the world—it impacts everything and everyone! And here are just a few reasons it is also one of the best career homes you could ever possibly choose.

1 Food Is Everywhere

There's a crazy truth about food we don't often consciously consider: Food is simply *everywhere* in our lives, throughout every day, hour by hour, sometimes even moment to moment. We think about it, long for it, look forward to it, plan it, read about it, talk about it, watch it on TV, start every morning with it, and end every evening with it. We even dream about it. It surrounds us in our thoughts and envelops us in our cravings, desires, and satisfaction, and it always leaves us thinking about what comes next. Even when a meal is terrible, it only makes us dream about all the times when those same ingredients were delicious.

When you honestly reflect on the good, the bad, and the ugly in your life—on all your most sacred memories, milestones, and even the places along the way that were catastrophically painful—guess what shows up there for all of it? That's right: food. (Okay, food and drink. *Definitely both.*) It's the candy bars and ham sandwiches you've grabbed at gas stations, the free coffee and powdered creamer sitting on the corner table at your bank, and all those times you drove through In-N-Out for your fave "secret recipe" burger. It's the orange slices on the soccer field you fought over as a kid—the ones that looked so dang refreshing as you pulled the ends of the wedges back with your fingers. It's the dinner in your future that you'll never forget, where an executive casually taps you on the shoulder for the job of your dreams (*Winning!*). It's even those Scrabble nights at home with almost regrettable amounts of booze, more friends than can fit at the table, and a complete spread, including a crazy-good and crazy-unexpected veggie salad with the best crispy wonton strips you've ever had in your life. *Yep, addictive salads are a real thing!* And it's also the sweet solitude of just sitting on the couch at home alone, watching a good show while you savor your favorite snack.

Let me stop right here and state the obvious: You can make a living from *any* of these food experiences. Cooking, party planning, food styling, grocery stocking, citrus farming, recipe writing, winemaking, supply sourcing, snack designing, birthday-cake baking—these are all jobs. And these jobs lead to other jobs. Better jobs. Bigger jobs!

Food *is* everywhere, yet for some insane reason, anyone who thinks about making a career here will face more than their fair share of naysayers. You don't see the big food companies recruiting at college campuses with the fanfare it deserves, you don't see food jobs ranking in any "hot career" lists, and—beyond those celebrity chefs and restaurateurs—you rarely see the interesting start-ups, the courageous innovators, or the big players featured in mainstream magazines. What you do see is a lot of negative stories about the industry as a place with limited career advancement and few meaningful work opportunities. I'm here to challenge that gap in a massive way because it is—in a word— some serious bullshit. I mean, there are very serious and real reasons why the food world gets the bad rap that it does. Frankly, in a lot of ways, the reputation is well deserved. *That is not a compliment.* But there is another side to this conversation that deserves a spotlight: the opportunity side of the food world and what it can mean for you. And while—absolutely yes—so much needs to evolve and change, we need to have the conversation about everything that is awesome, unique, and "right" about this industry, too. So, you can count on this book opening more than one Pandora's box throughout its pages, but I am also going to show you why pushing through it all can and will matter so significantly in your own life. After all, this book is entirely for you, and for your benefit.

If you want to see the real truth, just open your eyes and look around you. We're talking a *jaw-dropping* scale of opportunity. In the US alone, there are more than 330 million mouths to feed, each needing three square meals a day. That's around a billion meals daily, and it doesn't even include snack times, tourists, or even the second breakfast I like to eat on the weekends. That's some serious demand to meet just in this one country, and it takes a ton of people and lots of infrastructure to meet it.

So if you're looking for opportunity, it's here. Right in front of your mouth. So close you can taste it. You're already marinating in it, for crying out loud! So, wake up and smell the delicious magnitude of it all.

2 Food Is Full of People with High-Heat Passion

Let's say you're a big dreamer, bursting with ideas and a desire for change. Well, guess what? The food world is at the center of some of the most pressing, substantive, and critical environmental and social issues of our time. I'm talking trash and waste, chemical additives and food integrity, culture and equity, labor rights, animal welfare, environmental sustainability... and that's just to name a few. The opportunity to make the positive impact you want to see is literally all over the place— and you can guide yourself to those opportunities just by following your passions. Are you feeling me now?

"I Told You LEMONY Is a Scrabble Word!" Mega Veggie Party Salad with Crispy Wontons

ALL IN TAKES ABOUT 1 HOUR · ACTIVE TIME 45 MINUTES OVER 2 DAYS
MAKES 8 GENEROUS PORTIONS

This is the perfect salad for dinner parties because everything can be made in advance and it's super easy to assemble and serve. Want a cheffy tip? Defrost the wonton wrappers and fry them up the day before. If you place them in an airtight container with paper towels on the bottom to absorb any excess oil, you can hold these at room temp for several days. Makes assembling a breeze!

Kick-Ass Sesame-Soy Dressing

1 cup rice wine vinegar

½ cup + 1 tablespoon soy sauce

½ cup sesame oil

6 tablespoons organic canola or other vegetable oil

6 tablespoons dark brown sugar

1 tablespoon garlic, minced

Optional: 4 tablespoons chili sauce
Sriracha is my fave.

Crispy Pop-In-Your-Mouth Wonton Strips

1 package frozen wonton wrappers
You will need about 2 cups of fried wonton strips plus more for garnishing the salads.

3 cups organic canola or vegetable oil for frying the wonton wrapper strips

Yummy Crunchy Salad

You can save time by buying all the veg already shredded from your grocer.

6 ounces red cabbage, finely shredded

6 ounces green cabbage, finely shredded

6 ounces iceberg lettuce, shredded

4 ounces baby spinach

4 ounces carrot, shredded

3 ounces almonds, sliced and lightly toasted

2 10½-ounce cans mandarin oranges, drained and rinsed

¼ cup scallions, thinly sliced

Optional: mung bean sprouts and/or water chestnuts, sliced as desired

To make the dressing, whisk all dressing ingredients together until well incorporated. Adjust the flavor as desired (more sesame, more chili, etc.) and set in your fridge. *This part can hold up to 4 days in the fridge, so don't be afraid to make ahead!*

The day before you're ready to make the wonton strips, set the wrappers in the fridge to defrost overnight.

When you are ready to make the wonton strips, heat the frying oil in a saucepot over the stovetop to medium-high. Remove the wonton wrappers from packaging and slice into small strips. Test the oil temperature with one strip to make sure it's sizzling but not too hot/burning (approximately 350°F).

When the frying oil is hot, fry small batches of wonton strips until they bubble up and turn golden brown. Remove from the oil with a slotted metal spoon and let rest on a paper towel–lined plate. Once cool, store in airtight container lined with paper towels.

Right before you're ready to serve, assemble the salad. Prepare all the salad ingredients and add them to a large salad bowl. Add ¾ cup of your Kick-Ass Sesame-Soy Dressing and mix thoroughly. Taste and add more dressing if needed.

Portion the salad into salad bowls and garnish with a few fried wonton strips on top. Eat! *You can easily make a non-veggie version by adding your protein of choice: rotisserie chicken, shrimp, NY strip steak… the options are endless. It's all up to you!*

I mean, take my own story. I built my career by listening to my heart while I discovered what was important to me and what I enjoyed working on—and (read: especially!) what I didn't. This is a common experience for many who find themselves in food leadership: They follow their instincts and their joy, pay attention to what they love and don't love, and pivot accordingly. And as a result, they end up in wildly unexpected, unplanned places.

Think about how many young, passionate people find themselves in that headspace where they don't know what they want to do with their lives—in fact, you've probably even been there yourself, or you're there *right now*. It's so easy to get steeped in stress over not knowing, as if you're supposed to have some perfect, magical answer that guides you effortlessly like a beacon.

Truth is, most people I know have churned on this burning question at one point (or several!) in their lives. And I use the word "churn" for a reason: just look at butter. Milk needs a lot of friction to get to the creamy, luxurious buttery stage. That churn matters—it's a process, an evolution, a metamorphosis, and it's valuable—so when you find yourself churning, pay attention to that process because something will definitely be on the other side of it. Think about it: How many people do you know who have always had the one answer for what they want to do professionally? It's much more common to not know than to know—so, if that is you, trust me when I say you are in good company. The answers lie within you, and they will reveal themselves over time. Trust in that—*trust the churn*. You just have to pay attention to how you feel, moment to moment and even year to year.

Let's say you're super passionate about one thing—for example, really good bread. Imagine that you're working as a chef and you don't like any of the bread options available to serve with your meals, and it frustrates you so much that you decide to just make your own. And it turns out exactly how you wanted, so you open a small shop next door to the restaurant, borrow a friend's dining room table, and start selling your bread there along with a few open-faced sandwiches. Then you become so successful that you grow that business into a chain of more than 150 bakery restaurants in nineteen countries around the world. *All because you couldn't find a loaf of bread you liked.*

That is a true story, by the way—as told to me by Alain Coumont, who founded Le Pain Quotidien, now famous for those open-faced sandwiches, which are called "tartines." And I'm guessing that Mr. Coumont never imagined at the beginning, or even the middle, of his career that he would end up feeding millions. Or that he would drive global conversations around organic foods or be instrumental in creating awareness around the importance of reducing meat consumption and adopting plant-based diets. Quite a leap from his start in charcuterie, butter-based baked goods, and milk-based beverages, but, like everyone, he found himself growing, learning, and evolving. Mr. Coumont's newest restaurant concept, Le Botaniste, is a groundbreaking plant-based dining experience that combines a fast-casual approach with some of the most stunning dining spaces you will ever see. I mean, this guy is having a world of fun playing with "the possible" and using cutting-edge ideas and innovation to bring his food values to the world, one scrumptious, evolving bite at a time.

Or take Sweetgreen, another fast-casual concept that started in 2007 in Washington, DC, when three college friends struggled to find affordable, healthy, and delicious food options around campus. When they decided to open a restaurant and couldn't get funding, they borrowed $300,000 from a group of fifty friends and family members and had their first location opened within a few months of graduating. After not much more than a decade, their empire featured almost a hundred restaurants and had an IPO on the stock market with a valuation of $6 billion. I mean . . . *GTFO amazing.*

Sweetgreen is an example of what's possible when you put your effort into something you feel strongly about, and how that passion can fuel your ability to create a real impact. Hilariously, it's another example of people who created an amazing food brand all because of irritation over a gap. But that's the beauty of it: *when we strive to fix the things that bother us, that's when the progress begins.* Careers work exactly the same way: when you aren't satisfied with what you have, you move forward, and you do something about it.

Those Sweetgreen college-friends-turned-founders felt strongly about using their success to do good and find ways to "connect people with real food." That became their brand purpose, which ultimately turned a "creative salad in a bowl" concept into a magnetic social impact brand that works directly with schools to educate children on fresh, healthy food; partners with farmers to provide more transparency; and provides open information about their supply chain and ingredients. Talk about opportunity: to be able to drive the change you most want to see in the world is a privilege, and one that's enjoyed by the folks who stay in the game and fight for the chance to make that difference.

Others have joined the food world mid-career from other sectors and have gone on to make their own industry impact. Some of these leaders are even fueled by some pretty sizable "crash and burn" personal challenges from earlier on in their lives, only proving that no mistake or misstep should ever be big enough to derail your dreams. One of my favorite such food heroes is Sam Polk, the founder and CEO of Everytable in Los Angeles. He came from a place with no intersection with food at all—in fact, he was making crazy good money as a successful senior trader on Wall Street. But through his deeply personal journey with addiction and self-discovery, he came to recognize his own unique power to be a force for positive change—and to do it through the world of food. Polk used his skills and knowledge of the finance world to build a for-profit enterprise that is quickly becoming the new model for equitable franchise operations and affordable and healthy fast food. Everytable offers low-cost grab-'n'-go meals from restaurants and strategically placed smart fridges to supply both underserved communities and affluent neighborhoods. Their mission? "To transform the food system to make delicious, nutritious food accessible to everyone, everywhere." I mean, *how cool is that?* Polk has used his passion and most authentic self to create a world in which the cheapest food option is also the easiest to find *and* the most delicious and nutritious.

Everytable has also taken the learnings from the traditional franchising model to launch its Social Equity Franchise Program, which aims to assist people of color into franchise ownership through training, low-cost loans, and a guaranteed salary. I mean, just imagine this world where you can not only become a business owner and find personal success; you can also create opportunities for personal wealth and security *for others*—and all by way of a product offering that truly is good for bellies and communities. And here's the magic of churn for you: These amazing things happened not just *despite* Sam Polk's personal challenges, but *because* he was fueled by them. He took some of the hardest and most painful moments of his life and turned them into action and then impact . . . *for the better*.

This is the unique power of the food industry. It's a place full of unimaginable promise to create, inspire, enrich, and connect us all, one unstoppable bite at a time. That's the world I want to live in.

3 Food Is Where It Is All Up to You (Even If It Shouldn't Be)

Okay, let's talk about the most important ingredient in all of this: *you*. The biggest hurdle you are going to encounter in the food industry is your own capacity to see the significant, life-changing value in working your way up, one step at a time, even when that means from the ground floor. It's very likely that no one is going to fully show it to you—and later I'm going to get deep into why that is and why it sucks—but the upside of that is, once you understand this, you can basically write your own destiny.

Your success is dependent on you being able to see that your most worthwhile, important, and rich learnings will arrive not from what comes easily, but from all of your real-world experiences—especially the hard stuff. You can take this news from me directly: my own first jobs in the industry were low-wage and grueling, and, yes, some were totally wild (like catering for the porn industry—another book, another time!). And there's worse to admit, too: some of my early jobs left me feeling degraded, demoralized, and depressed more days than not. But those challenges, as awful as they were, were eclipsed by the opportunities that kept opening up to me. Sure, it took more than a few tries to get there; I had many "new starts," most of which you'll hear about over the course of this book. And when, at the age of twenty-four, I realized I wanted to become a "real" chef after years of working odd jobs, learning the ropes, and eventually finding really good financial success in some unexpected corners of the industry, I basically started all over—again!—and headed to Paris and Le Cordon Bleu to learn how to cook from the best.

As I worked my way back up through the ranks, I ran restaurants, developed recipes that have been served all over the globe, and traveled the world. I ended up directing the food and beverage teams for two major international food brands—Pret A Manger in the US and Le Pain Quotidien in the US, France, and eventually for the global master franchise. I went from being in charge of ten employees in my first kitchen management role to overseeing more than 1,200 across forty-plus restaurants serving around 60,000 meals a day for Google through the Bon Appétit Management Company. Today, I run my own consulting company, helping food organizations and their teams achieve their goals (involving food programs, menu and recipe development, operational and organizational solutions—you know, pretty much everything to do with food!), and I coach and counsel teams and executives throughout it all.

None of this would have happened had I not stuck it out and consistently brought my best self to whatever it was I was asked to do—even when the job was bad. Even when it was more than bad! And even when it meant that my best self wasn't yet at its best. It absolutely kills me that so many junior food-industry employees are missing this opportunity to build their own future and expand their capacity in the same way. Young people entering the industry think there is no opportunity beyond their current, low-paying job, and so they leave. Or they think those demoralizing moments in their job—of which there are always too many—are just too damn hard to endure, especially in light of sometimes appalling compensation. Even worse: they stay but don't bring their A-game, which ensures they won't move up. And I don't just see this at the entry level! Even managers can behave this way, never realizing they're shooting themselves in the foot career-wise.

And here's where I open the first Pandora's box: In my experience, the poor communication that exists around what these jobs can really unlock in your career rests largely in the hands of employers. The simple truth is that employers are *stewards* of the careers of everyone on their payroll for as long as those careers—and lives!—are in their hands.

Employers are finally beginning to understand this holistic responsibility and put it demonstrably into practice. To be a good steward of someone's career simply means being in service to them while they are in service to you. Employers who practice this core philosophy—and whose leaders authentically care about each team member's experiences and goals—earn and harness the collective power of their team in extraordinary ways. *I am talking about seriously enhanced performance.*

Career development is about gaining skills, experience, tools, maturity, social and emotional growth, and a thousand other things. Your ability to personally and professionally grow and thrive impacts everything—your life, your colleagues, and your employer. In a perfect world, the responsibility for unlocking these mysteries around personal, individual (I'm talking about *you*) career development would sit with your employers, but for whatever inexplicable reason, and despite the thirst for employees who will value their organizations and become loyal, dedicated workers for many years, personal career development has not been a part of provided learning in most food companies, especially within the entry, beginning, and middle management roles. It boggles my mind because these roles are the most likely to drive a company's performance. What you personally impact in these jobs matters significantly to your employer and its overall financial outcomes.

Sure, there's a lot of employer investment in training when it comes to delivering the responsibilities of the day-to-day roles, but up until now, rarely has there been actual one-on-one or group conversations intended to crack open the incredible reserves of *individual* passion and ambition that exists within the people working in this industry—nor has there been a clear menu or road map provided for where *you* can go and what *you* can achieve if only you learned or did X or Y within your organization. Remember how I said that so much innovation in the food world is sparked by irritation over a gap? Well, guess why I wrote this book. (And trust me—I'm not just talking to you. As you read this, I am furiously writing a whole separate book to deliver this message directly to leaders and employers. It is long past time for them to loudly demonstrate their career stewardship commitment and highlight the unique investments they are making for their workforce's benefit.)

It took me quite a while to identify this flaw in the system for myself, but as I reached more senior levels of leadership and began to learn about what was available in terms of training and development tools, I became mystified by how little employers were investing in sharing tools and resources to support *all* levels of career growth across the organization, especially the entry and management levels. I also always assumed that because I didn't go to college, "career development" was a class I surely missed, and as I figured things out over the years about work dynamics, or as mentors shared personal stories or advice and a light bulb went off in my head, I quietly thought, so many times, *Why didn't anyone ever tell me that? Gah!* I have since learned that career development isn't actually taught in most school curriculums as a dedicated "thing." Unless you are 1) aware that it is even a thing that exists, 2) ambitious and curious enough to figure out where to look for it and what to expect from it, or 3) your employer is investing in it on your behalf for the mutual benefit of both of you, career development is just not a mainstream conversation. At least, not yet—not until you and I fight for the change this industry needs.

So, until that change comes, you are going to have to be ambitious and curious enough to figure this out on your own. I'm here to give you a leg up with the most important lesson you need right now: the food world is all about *performance.* You will get out of it what you put into it, and I can say with 100 percent certainty that if you bring your A-game to a low-paying hourly job, you will absolutely move up. If you want to get into management, you will. If you want to move from management to leadership, you will. How do I know this? Because I have seen it firsthand again and again.

Fully understanding this can feel tough (*hard work ahead!*), but it can also feel liberating (*nothing can stop you but you!*). Coming from a different industry? No problem. Whatever skills you have, they're needed in the food world. Have a college degree in art, business, anything at all? Amazing! (And congrats on your incredible achievement!) Whatever you learned will come in handy at some point. And if you don't have a degree, then let me tell you something: *Over half* of Americans have never graduated from college. Way more than half, in fact—two-thirds! That's a massive number of people working in all kinds of industries who never got the benefit of an academic relationship network or the knowledge gleaned from professors, classmates, courses, and studies. There are more people like us in the workforce than those with a degree. More "students of life" than actual students. I personally think that's pretty cool and something you can be proud of. Nothing can or will stop you from achieving your dreams in this industry—you just have to be willing to do the work. And, yes, do some demanding, low-paying jobs for a while.

It doesn't even matter where or who you are in life. Julia Child was forty-nine when her first cookbook was published—and that was after a whole other career in government services, and a ton of rejection and "failure." Food welcomes everyone, regardless of background, experience, and education, and regardless of demographics, too. Just look at the stats: in the US alone, there are more women and minority managers working in this industry than in any other, and nine in ten restaurant managers started in entry-level positions.

The food world is *the* place where you can earn your way to fulfilling your career dreams, because performance matters above anything else. If you can bring your talent and effort to everything you do, the extraordinary achievements and career advancement you will unlock are beyond anything you can imagine. And that is truly a beautiful thing. And when it's your turn at the top, my guess is that you will make our industry more supportive of its workers. Honestly, I'm counting on it, and I'm rooting for you! And it's my mission to help you make your way through it all so that you can use your influence for good when you finally reach the leadership roles with the authority to truly create impact.

4 Food Is Love

And that brings us to the final thing that is absolutely, unequivocally, and beautifully right about this world. If you're reading this book, then you adore food. And that means there was probably a moment in your life when a meal was placed in front of you and everything about it was simply magnificent. Maybe it looked gorgeous. Or maybe it was a hot mess! Either way, there was something so compelling about the texture and colors. It smelled like heaven. And when you put that first bite in your mouth, you thought, *I cannot believe how insanely delicious this is. My mind is literally blown.*

And if that experience was wrapped up in a gathering of family and friends, then right there you understood that food was about love. And if food is about love, then food is about *life*.

For me, my first moments like that happened with my grandmother Emilie—who famously didn't cook, except that she secretly did when I was with her. Growing up with divorced parents, I spent part of my year in Los Angeles and part in the Midwest with my dad and Emilie. While he was off working for the railroad, Emilie and I would make all sorts of things together. To be completely fair, you wouldn't really call most of it "cooking"—it was more the "assembling of cooked things." There was rarely chopping, measuring, or even making a mess, other than what we dropped or spilled.

Sometimes we had Le Menu frozen dinners, which she had a bizarre and curious taste for, or her famous "cheesy-egg" (as I called it), where she would fry an egg sunny-side up in a seriously tiny green Le Creuset frying pan and place exactly one perfect square of American cheese directly on top so that it melted in that kind of tacky, plastic, wrinkled effect that signaled it was hot and oozy enough to eat. Most meals, including cheesy-egg for breakfast, were finished with the smallest scoop of Häagen-Dazs Rum Raisin in a delicate scalloped crystal bowl with a dainty spoon. It was so ridiculously over the top: American cheese and crystal!

Our most memorable meals by far were the lobsters, which we would get from the fish guy over on LaSalle. We would circle around the box of those sad little lobsters with anticipation and dread as they blew tiny "I'm dying" bubbles from their faces. My grandmother would chug glasses of Bolla Soave wine in order to build up the courage to plunk them headfirst into the boiling pot and hold the lid down as they struggled to be free once they realized their fate. (Years later, in culinary school, I would learn the humane way to do it, with a quick plunging knife to the neck, but in the 1980s, boiling was pretty standard.) We would both scream and holler while she held the lid in place and I would run around the kitchen screeching and cry-laughing because we were just so fraidy-scared of the lobsters, and we were murderers, and it was all such drama. I mean, those suckers are strong, and they would really put up a fight sometimes; it was just brutal and very intense. But man, when we finally got to eat them—split down the middle with small porcelain ramekins full of frothy melted butter and a bunch of lemon wedges on the side—they were *so* delicious that we would instantly forget about our crimes of carnage.

Emilie had lived a full and privileged life, and so our meals together were complete with a treasure trove of European linens, fine china, and antique silver, some of which she had acquired from her years as the wife of a Navy lieutenant (and later captain). While we cooked, she told me stories about the places she went, the people she met, and the experiences she'd had, and she showed me all the ways to set the table properly for breakfast, lunch, high tea, dinner, and dessert, with so many different utensils and serving pieces. In my mind, it was like living in Martin Scorsese's movie *The Age of Innocence*, though in reality it was a lot more like *Grey Gardens*. Emilie's home was where I first learned that presentation was part of what elevates the rituals of life.

I didn't realize it at the time, but those dinners and experiences were deeply formative in terms of my future life and career. Those moments made me feel full of joy, wonder, and possibility. Emilie ignited my curiosity around food, even when she was doing horrific things like sprinkling liquid smoke on microwaved burger patties to create the most putrid smell ever to infiltrate human nostrils. (Not joking—I'm scarred for life.) These moments created not only joy, connection, and vibrant playfulness for me, but also an overall awareness of all the ways that life happens *around* food. I knew I wanted to travel and see and taste the world, and to visit all the places I had heard about from my Emilie, especially Europe. What I didn't know then was that any of this was a viable *career* option. It literally never crossed my mind in those early days.

But now that I have been in the business for decades and made my life here, I know that working in food is *all* about love. It's about bringing people together to celebrate and commiserate, to toast and mourn. It's about nourishment and sustenance, not just of the body but of the spirit, too.

Where there is food, there is love. And food is everywhere! And you can make a career in it, using nothing more than your incredible self! That's pretty amazing. Now let's find out how to get started.

TIME TO GET INTO MISE MODE

**The prep you need to imagine everything
available to you in the world of food.**

MINDSET SHIFT: Your career journey is in *your* hands. There are many entry points swirling around you, so pay attention to all the places that might offer a career that will deliver on what you want for yourself. That means paying attention to what matters to you—and especially the "churn" you feel along the way.

TRADE SECRET: The food world is a place where you have the power to earn your way to your own dreams, *because personal performance matters above anything else.*

LEADERSHIP LOWDOWN: Yes, you can work in food and change the world. The greatest leaders in this industry write their own rules for what a successful business should look like, and what role it can play in improving the lives of not just their teams but also entire communities.

⭐ INSIDER DISH

*More incredible insights
here—check it out!*

2

YES, YOU HAVE TO EAT YOUR LIMA BEANS BEFORE DESSERT

Getting to the Great Stuff, One "Crumby" Job at a Time

This is you putting yourself and your dreams first. **Because if you won't do that, who will?**

LET'S BE REAL: Your first job in the world of food is probably going to, well, suck. It's going to have less-than-exciting pay, and, oh, it's going to be grueling, too. In fact, entry-level positions in the food industry can be some of the hardest jobs in the world for what's often the worst compensation imaginable. Rather than entry-level jobs, they should maybe be called "extraordinary effort required in challenging, stressful conditions for disgracefully low pay" jobs. Don't even get me started on what I think about this and how fully unnecessary it is. It is the current reality, however, and for all these reasons, yes, these jobs can suck. But (and this is a *big* but) your early-career jobs are also the "trail of bread-crumbs" you need to follow in order to reach the job of your dreams. So, let's call them "crumby" jobs. Flaky, messy, sometimes falling apart and all over the place, but always leading you forward. And unlike for Hansel and Gretel, they will actually get you where you want to go.

When I was starting out in the food industry as a teenager, I was passionate about cooking and loved having dinner parties—it brought me back to those early meals with Emilie, my grandmother. My living conditions in those first scrappy years on my own were simple, but somehow I was able to entertain anyway. I cherished experimenting with recipes and was obsessed with making chicken Milanese (yep— more breadcrumbs!), except I made mine with turkey breast and tons of lemon, and I called it my "dinner party obsession." I can still smell the scent of the nutty, crackling butter mixing with the citrus as I cut up the lemons. My absolute favorite. I still use lemons every day. And butter. Because life is too short not to enjoy good butter.

All the planning that went into the parties was my absolute jam. I would get inspiration for what to make and how to present it from places like *Gourmet* magazine and *The Joy of Cooking*. I read cookbooks like they were novels and had more culinary fails than you can imagine over those years. Embarrassing "Cooking 101" things, like not knowing that I had to devein shrimp before serving shrimp cocktail, or making perfect pan-sautéed filet mignon steaks (with garlicky mushrooms!) that were beautifully seared and scrumptious looking on the outside, but totally raw on the inside. There is literally nothing worse than presenting dinner to much fanfare and then having all your friends cringe at the food. Oh, the shame of it all!

Even when I got the food right, I struggled with timing. Why was timing so damn hard? Why couldn't I have everything hot and ready at the same time? I felt like I was always running to have the food served as an actual meal and not an unintentionally coursed experience. Voilà! Green beans. And five minutes later, ta-da! Turkey Milanese. And five minutes later, a chaser of mashed potatoes!? But with those fails came all the laughs, gaffes, and my most precious memories, because while learning about cooking and serving, I also learned to cherish the joy of sharing and connecting with others.

My Story of Waking Up and Growing Up

When I was a teen, I got a job with a company called California Pizza Kitchen, which had taken Los Angeles by storm. It was a big deal, because it meant good tips and fantastic perks (like awesome food to eat). I went into CPK "school" for a week, passed the training, got onto the dining floor—and realized immediately how uncomfortable I was in front of other people. I was *so* nervous, carrying the food, trying to remember orders, and, through it all, desperately trying to "act natural." I lasted a week. I still remember going home to my tiny apartment after I was fired and making Noodles Romanoff from a box (I had no stove, just a microwave and a hot plate). I felt like a failure, I needed comfort, and that meant I needed buttery noodles. *Stat.*

I thought I was through with restaurant life, and that cooking from that point forward would be limited to entertaining at home—I mean, restaurant life was so hard! Because I was already on my own at that time in my life and I had quit high school, I was making ends meet by working odd jobs while slowly building a side hustle helping small companies manage their books. Like so many others, I was winging it every day.

ARMED WITH a fake ID that I had procured from an enterprising employee through a well-known fast-food company's drive-through window (yes, the folks working the ordering window offered a "side" of faux documents... you know, back in the days before anything was digitized), I spent eighteen months of my life jumping between odd jobs and working in Hollywood nightclubs. I'll be honest: I wasn't exactly a model employee. I liked to party and play, and I saw work as just a means to an end. I never thought about building a career or having a future in, well... anything. I was just surviving, trying to pay my bills, and intent on having a good time.

But one day I woke up and realized that I was searching for something more, and that I hadn't gone through all those tough times just to end up as some lame-ass party girl. So, I cleaned up my act and started to get serious about how I was going to build my life. I was nineteen at that point and had no real idea about what to do. I had grown up in what I call "the in-between": While my grandparents had been wealthy and successful, my parents were professionally and financially "challenged," leaving me in this strange ecosystem of access to privileges like grandparent-funded private schooling and country clubs on the one hand, and a home existence of scraping by and barely paying bills on the other. It left me with no real-life, day-to-day modeling of what it takes to work hard and build something financially stable. But it also gave me an understanding of what having money and resources can mean in terms of quality of life, security, and freedom.

"Dinner Party Obsession"
Buttery Lemon Turkey Milanese

ALL IN TAKES ABOUT 25 TO 30 MINUTES • ACTIVE TIME 20 MINUTES
SERVES 4 HUNGRY PEOPLE

Typically, you can find this on menus served with a brightly seasoned fresh salad—I love to eat it that way... I also love to eat it with Noodles Romanoff or potato mash or all sorts of other things. Eat it however you like!

---

4 to 8 turkey breast cutlets
Depends on the size of the cuts!

1 teaspoon Maldon sea salt flakes

4 to 5 turns fresh black pepper

1 cup all-purpose flour

3 eggs, whisked well with a fork

1½ cups panko breadcrumbs

Mix together with flour, Maldon, and black pepper to make a seasoned flour.

½ to 1 cup unsalted butter,
at room temperature, if possible

More Maldon salt and black
pepper to season the raw meat
And also for after it's cooked!

2 lemons, washed and quartered

On a cutting board with plastic wrap below and on top of the turkey breast cutlets, flatten them until they're about ½ inch thick by pounding them with the bottom of a heavy frying pan.

Put the whisked eggs, seasoned flour, and panko breadcrumbs into three separate bowls.

Season both sides of the turkey breasts with Maldon salt and black pepper, and then, one at a time, follow this flour/egg/breadcrumb assembly-line process: 1) Dip the cutlet in the flour until evenly coated. Shake off any excess flour, and 2) dip the floured cutlet in the eggs and shake off any excess before placing it in the breadcrumbs to evenly coat the entire turkey breast.

Place the cutlets on a plate and cover with plastic wrap until you are ready to cook them. You can do this up to 24 hours in advance without losing quality. It's a real time-saver!

When you're ready to eat, heat up half the butter in a frying pan. Over medium heat, lightly sauté the turkey until the breadcrumbs are golden brown all over—about 2 to 3 minutes on each side. *You may need to add more butter throughout the cooking process to make sure the meat is all evenly cooked, so keep it close by.*

Once the cutlets are done, add to a plate and sprinkle a touch of Maldon salt to the top and a generous squeeze of lemon. Serve with lemon quarters and Maldon on the side!

What I couldn't see then was that those "crumby," low-paying, super-stressful jobs were leading me to that point of maturity. Truthfully, I actively regretted those years for a long time, but the lessons I learned in those hourly roles and the experiences I had at the bottom rung of the industry were so impactful and life-changing that, from where I stand today, I can't even imagine my career having gone the way it did without those challenges and growing pains. Those years were grueling and exhausting, but they were also rich with opportunities to learn, gather skills, grow up, and prepare myself for the challenges I would face as I made my way up the career ladder. They made me realize not only that I wanted more for my life, but also that I was capable and deserving of more.

Perhaps the biggest gift those jobs gave me was the early realization that *no one* in the world actually gave a shit about my career in the same way I did. It is so important for you to embrace this jolting truth in its full, difficult, uncomfortable glory, so let me really lay it down for you now: *No one in the world is going to give a shit about your career in the same way you do.* Literally not one person! I mean, sure, your family and friends will want your happiness and satisfaction at work, and you'll have genuine supporters, bosses, and mentors along the way who will root for your success, be your advocate, and steer you through many of the barriers and problems you encounter. But really, no one in the whole world will be as affected by or invested in your career journey or the hardships you will experience as you are. That rests in *your* heart and on *your* shoulders alone.

That's why it's personal.

That's why all of this matters so much.

It's how you spend your days, your blood, sweat, and tears, your energy and efforts; and it starts and ends with you by way of your personal decisions and actions.

I found delicious freedom and so much promise in this truth along the way. *Your personal career journey rests in your heart and on your shoulders alone.* That's some powerful stuff right there. And if you take the long view and understand that any challenging career moment you encounter (and there will be many)—whether you're cleaning gum off a restaurant table for the umpteenth time or sweating it out in the endless eighth hour of the steamy dish pit—will lead you where you want to go, you will feel that same freedom and promise, too.

Meet Your New Best Friend: Your Resilience Muscle

Okay—we've established that entry-level food jobs can be low-paying and tough. But wait, there's more! They can also be stressful, urgent, dangerous, and deeply complicated. You will find yourself dealing with folks who are impatient, rude, and even a little "cray-cray." If you work in a warehouse, food processing plant, or restaurant, you will be on your feet for most of the day. Actually, the whole damn day.

You will deal with challenging bosses—some who will push you for better performance and sharper skills, and some who are straight-up assholes. *Things should be easier,* you will tell yourself. But that's not reality. Your work—and your life, for that matter—doesn't really get easier. *You* get better. And as you learn and get more experience, you will become more skilled at dealing with those challenges.

The thing is, you'll find most of these issues in any industry, on any day of the week, and at every single level of your career. These provocations are not exclusive to the world of food. But what is unique about the food industry is that, no matter your background or education, you can actually *work* your way up from the lowest-level "crumbiest" job, learn the skills and grab the tools, and earn your entry into management. And then from management into leadership. It really is all available to you. Yes, it will be hard, and, yes, many of you who are reading this are already carrying the unbelievable weight on those same hearts and shoulders that will have to take on this effort, too. But each of us has the ability to choose to strive for something different, and to recognize that the desire for better is noble, and that we are worthy of the work it takes.

It's up to each of us, individually. You need to commit to yourself that you are not going to let anyone or anything get in your way of achieving your dreams. Think about it: If no one actually gives a shit about your career, why would you let someone else knock you out of the game? *Why would you give anyone or anything that power over you?*

See what I mean? It's all about you—about what you are willing to endure and what will be unlocked if you have the staying power to see it through. A future full of promise, potential, and reward. A pathway to continued growth and opportunity. A future transition from an hourly wage to a salary and from a salary to making a comfortable living. Labor to management. Management to leadership. And, in the end, making *your* dreams happen. That's what you get when you push through the "crumby" jobs. They are the invisible gateway to the future you have been dreaming about.

True, it's going to take more than a minute to fix what's broken around these entry-level jobs and the hardships they entail. In the meantime, *mindset* will see you through. Mindset matters significantly when it comes to your own career development—it is the heart of working in Mise Mode. It's character, determination, self-respect, fortitude, the ability to find worth in challenge—and the capacity to recognize all of these aspects. It's holding yourself as the most precious and important factor in every twist and turn—*your* joy, *your* purpose, *your* dreams. It all matters. *You* matter.

Remember those stories I told you about Everytable and Sweetgreen and all the other food leaders who reached amazing positions of influence and leadership just by following their passions? They weren't particularly special or unique in what drove them. We all have things we feel passionate or irritated about. What sets them apart is their relentless drive and determination in pursuit of their dreams. They all pushed through extraordinary challenges, big "failures" (read: opportunities to learn), and massive roadblocks, but they didn't let those things get in the way. They stayed the course, even though they had no idea where the road would lead. They all had a serious, committed "I'm going to figure it out" mindset. *They saw it through.*

What these leaders also had—and what you have, too, somewhere inside you—is a muscle called *resilience*. If you want to reach the same kind of success they reached, it's time to start working that muscle out every day. You will need this muscle to be big and strong. There will be many moments when you don't feel like you're making progress. You will deal with unhappy customers, and colleagues who don't pull their share, and bosses who are mean and unfair. Expect this. Each of these moments is an opportunity to *not* let it knock you over. That's your daily workout, the reps you lift to build that muscle. Keep your eyes on the prize, and you will soon see that you are learning, improving, and developing your own unique style—a distinction you will need as you move up the ladder and into supervisory roles, management, and eventually executive leadership. It is all about building blocks and setting the foundation at this stage. You are at the beginning of your journey. Now is the time to pay your dues and learn as much as you possibly can. Keep pushing, practice your resilience, and focus on where it will take you.

I once supervised an incredibly talented young man who had worked his way up from the bottom of a global culinary operation based in France to become a general manager in New York City. After I left that business to join another, he was put through some intense and unpleasant "asks" from his leadership that felt unreasonable and, frankly, outrageously disrespectful. Let me put it this way: He would have been fully justified in quitting his job. He reached out to me a few times to discuss these issues, but he always ended up choosing to stay because he loved the people he worked with. He actively focused on what he enjoyed about the work, and that carried him through the endless difficulties. Years later, he became a partner at a well-respected, cutting-edge food concept, all because of the strength of the relationships he developed while working through those hard times. Today, that man is living his career dreams—as a business owner in the field he loves—because he didn't let the unpleasantness of a given moment knock him out of the game. He had one heck of a resilience muscle. And he had it because he *exercised* it.

By the way, I know this is super hard, and that it can feel like all you're doing is swallowing a ton of BS. It can be totally tempting to just quit. I've been there, and I've been talking to my teams about exercising their resilience muscle since the mid-2000s. But if you're feeling doubtful about anything I'm saying here, check out Sheryl Sandberg and Adam Grant's 2017 book, *Option B: Facing Adversity, Building Resilience, and Finding Joy.* They talk about resilience in a similar, more detailed way.

"If It Was Easy, Everyone Would Do It"

I used to think of this mantra every time I was frustrated or wanted to quit (which was sometimes daily!). Not everyone will stick it out, but that just opens the field for those of us who do. One of the most important things I learned during my time in the trenches was that exercising my resilience muscle brought me a lot of rewards, including greater learnings. I just didn't want to fail. That would have been even more humiliating than the things I had to endure—the naysayers would have been right. *Nope, that was definitely not happening.* It's easy to quit. Much harder to stay. Learning how to do that when things get tough has been a gift to my career, just as it will be for yours.

And you won't be alone. So many people have come into the food world from places of deep hardship and personal challenge and gone on to build extraordinary things they never imagined were possible. *All fueled by personal willpower.* I mean, imagine finding yourself recently divorced and jobless in your early thirties and deciding to go back to school to start all over again. Then, on one sunny, ordinary day, you're hiking up the Colorado Mountains and you realize that the trail mix you have on hand isn't cutting it. What you're longing for is a portable energy bar that is really indulgent, truly healthy and deeply satisfying, and made from real ingredients. So, when you get back home to your tiny kitchen, you grab your food processor and some almonds, dates, and cherries and start to play with the idea. And before you know it, you have a few recipes you love. Jump forward a few years and your brand has been bought by General Mills for tens of millions of dollars.

That's the story of Lara Merriken, founder of LÄRABAR, one of the best-selling energy bars in America (Cherry Pie is my fave, in case you're wondering). Talk about personal willpower. As for me, I can tell you with certainty that as a high school dropout who once found herself setting up a beautiful catered lunch for a bunch of hungry, half-naked porn industry workers in the San Fernando Valley, I never, ever, would have imagined that I would end up working with people from all over the world, overseeing the food and beverage programs for major brands, and building my own consulting firm. Not in my wildest dreams. I was just happy to be able to pay my rent and work in the field I loved. But as my awareness for "the possible" grew, so did my ambition, and then so did my dreams.

That's the curious thing about dreams: they unfold in mysterious ways and reveal themselves in those unexpected, unplanned moments. "That job sounds cool" or "I want to work for that company because I like the concept" or "I want to make something because I see a need and an opportunity" always leads to something incredibly worthwhile. But to get to those moments, you have to commit to the path. Careers are made one step at a time—job by job, decision by decision, breadcrumb by breadcrumb. Being brave, paying your dues, taking the learnings as well as the guff, and staying in the game are the only secrets to success at this critical early stage. Those commitments will allow you to push yourself up into the next level and see where you might be able to go from there, all the while unlocking each role and work experience like gateways on the path.

Unbearable Moments Now
Can Be Hilarious Memories Later

You are going to leave some regrets behind you on your path. It's a long road, so it can't be helped! But your resilience muscle can help you make the right choices in stressful moments so that you keep those potholes to a minimum. Be kind to yourself and be kind to others. Especially when your boss is scolding you, when your coworkers are dropping the ball, or when your customers are being horrendous. We so often focus on the negative experiences because they take more effort and are harder to navigate and process. We can take difficult moments personally (I mean, they *are* personal—it's happening to us,

FFS!), which makes them tough to shake off. I have found over the years that the trick is to actively remember the relaxed, delightful, enjoyable experiences simultaneously, because they happen all the time. And those terrible, horrible, awful experiences? They often become quite funny with some time and distance. You will laugh, cry, and bond with old friends over these stories all through your lifetime.

Take one guy in an El Pollo Loco chicken outfit who spent some of his early working days standing on the sidewalk, sweating in his feathered costume and waving a "Grand Opening" sign to get the attention of drivers, who just honked and flipped him the bird. If you'd seen this poor soul, you'd have felt bad for him, thinking that he probably hated his job and was desperate for cash. Years later, do you think the guy remembers that job fondly and tells great stories about those days? Yep—he sure does. I know this because that's the story Brad Pitt told to Ellen DeGeneres on her TV show. Everyone starts somewhere—even Brad Pitt. "Man's gotta eat" and "no shame," he proudly shared with Ellen. But if you had asked him how he felt about that job at the time, I have a hunch his comments might not have been so positive.

(That said, maybe you know someone who is struggling with their career in a very real way. If that's the case, I sincerely want to help, too. Go to atasteofopportunity.com right now—I've given directions for bonus resources that I think can really help with navigating, well, all the things: insights, inspiration, and lots of Mise Mode goodness. *It truly does take a village, and we are all in this together!*)

My point is that there will be *many* tough moments over the course of your career. The one thing that will be consistently true through it all is that it's all on you to decide how to handle them. If you decide to lean on your resilience muscle—if you keep your personal goals top of mind and use them as fuel to make it through—then there is no end to what you can achieve. This is not some Jedi-level mind mastery stuff here; this is you putting yourself and your dreams first. Because if you won't do that, who will?

In the food world, it's up to you to decide how big and bold you want to go. The time has come for you to imagine the possibilities and allow yourself this moment to grab on to the reality that *you can have any future you want for yourself in this industry.* Your forever story and all your dreams for freedom, money, security, opportunity, and a chance to be a part of a bigger conversation, and even to change the world, can all be achieved here. And it doesn't matter what brought you to this moment. Here you are.

So, how bad do you want the life you think you want? When you realize what's possible, it will wash over you like a cool and tangy Michelada with a Tajín-spiced rim on a hot summer day and keep you refreshed for the hard stuff ahead. Drink up, friend—because it's time to get to work.

TIME TO GET INTO MISE MODE

**Your prep for toughing out the "crumby" jobs
and seeing the trail they're building for you.**

MINDSET SHIFT: There's the frustration and pain of right now, and then there's the wisdom and gratitude of the long road. Exercise your resilience muscle to move your mind out of the hard moments and into the longer view.

TRADE SECRET: Remember: "If it was easy, everyone would do it." Folks who are in it for the long game use their personal goals as fuel to overcome those deeply challenging moments. It's easy to quit, much harder to stay. But this is *your* life. What do *you* want to achieve? By staying and accumulating knowledge and experience, you are already on your way to what's next.

LEADERSHIP LOWDOWN: When you truly grasp that no one cares about your career as much as you do, you come to realize that this thought isn't depressing, it's *liberating*. You are in control of where you want to go and what you're willing to do to get there.

INSIDER DISH

*Whoa—another code?
More insights? Heck yeah!*

3

THE NEXT JOB AFTER YOUR FIRST JOB

How and When to Make Your Move

Half of the art of moving ahead is **walking through an open door when one is presented to you.**

REMEMBER MY TEENAGE JOB experience at California Pizza Kitchen and how I turned out to be the worst server in recorded history? If your early experiences with the industry were as rocky as mine, you must never forget that the food world is so much bigger than you can imagine. I thought maybe I was done with this industry forever after I was fired at CPK, but it found me again, only this time in a completely different corner.

On a serendipitous whim, I started working for an agricultural commodities broker who was an old high school friend of my uncle's. He sold processed ingredients to food manufacturers out of his home office (a workplace that came complete with two high-energy boxer dogs). It was a whole new world of mass-produced food, which I had never thought about before. One customer we worked with made ten thousand pies a day out of a facility in Torrance, California. I had seen and eaten my fair share of pies from the grocery store over the years—we're all familiar with those stacks of pumpkin pies you see in the stores at Thanksgiving—but I had never stopped to think about where they actually came from. Ten thousand pies! *A day!* I needed to learn more because all I could think about was Willy Wonka. But real life. With pies!

I ended up working with that broker for the next five years, learning the purchasing side of the food business and selling products like egg, dairy, and vegetable powders to manufacturers like Edy's, Contadina, and Keebler. It was literally a penny business. For some products, we made a couple of cents a pound, others even a quarter-penny per pound. But when you sell forty thousand pounds at two cents profit, you make $800 for that one truckload. *And I sold a lot of truckloads.* So, by the time I was twenty, I was on my way to making a very comfortable living.

I also learned a lot about food safety, transportation, supply chains, and all the financial controls around mass-produced food. My favorite part of the job was coordinating LTL deliveries (that's "less-than-truckload") and negotiating the costs with one particular warehouse owner in Los Angeles, who always gave me good deals and told hilarious jokes. *(Thanks, Dave!)* When I visited his team at the warehouse, it felt like another world—all the truckers and their massive 18-wheelers dropping off, loading up, and barreling by. The warehouse was enormous, spotless, and buzzing, and it was so exciting to be in the middle of it. I had never considered that someone could have a successful and satisfying career dealing in the storage and logistics of food. A whole new universe was cracking open for me.

In my time there, I also learned a lot about ingredients I never knew existed, and things like how the dried, frozen, and liquid products we worked with were pasteurized so they could be stored for months and were designed to be produced in such a way that pricing could be held for a quarter of a year or more if a company was willing to contract that far out. Lots were. Some of the products we dealt with were ingredients sold in fifty-pound sacks and with shelf lives that lasted longer than anyone would want to hear about.

I was stunned by the bizarre things some products contained, like food additives that were actually "heat activated encapsulated smells," developed to intentionally deceive the human senses. Have you ever noticed that the strangest thing happens when the powdered mix in some packaged macaroni-and-cheese products reaches a certain temperature in the pot? Out of the blue, a certain smell arrives, seemingly from out of nowhere, that completely ignites your taste buds and hunger pangs. It just hits you like a freight train. Suddenly, you're overwhelmed by a smell that is so gorgeous, rich, cheesy, and pasta-y that you cannot wait to shove that macaroni in your mouth. And then you do. And it tastes like old, soppy cardboard that's been sitting on a sidewalk all day in the sun. Flat, gross, and disgusting. So why did it smell so damn good? *WTF is going on here?* Well. Let's just say that there is more than cheese in that recipe. Like I said, I learned a lot . . . just search online for "microencapsulation" if you want to learn about it, too.

In my time at that brokerage, I also learned that, as energizing as I found the business, I *hated* making cold calls—the kind where you have to call someone who has no interest in talking to you and get them to buy your stuff. I would get nervous and sweaty and spend hours talking myself into them. I realized that if I was going to stay in the field, that's what I would eventually be doing all the time. *Ugh.* I felt way more comfortable behind the scenes, so I knew it was time to look for a change.

"Forward" Can Mean Sideways (or Even Backward)

We all think we know what "career" means. Most people think it's a noun—the one word for all the jobs we work in progression over the course of our lives. What we don't often discuss is that "career" is a verb, too—and I mean that literally, from the dictionary: "to move fast and in a way that is out of control" or "to move swiftly and in an uncontrolled way in a specified direction." I love "career" as a combination of the noun and the verb because *it is so dang true.* You are in this for the long game—you know, like, *forever.* Life can be looooong, and career journeys can be very unpredictable. That means you always want to pay attention to what you are learning at any given moment, and especially how you are feeling as you're learning it. What dreams are your current work experiences sparking in you? What "hunger for next" is igniting that fire in your belly? Maybe it's just a gnawing feeling that's unshakeable no matter how much you try to ignore it. You know that something else is waiting for you, and you know you have to be bold and brave enough to take the leap if you're going to meet it. That was my experience.

Macaroni and Cheese
Not from a box!

ALL IN TAKES ABOUT 40 MINUTES · ACTIVE TIME 25 MINUTES
MAKES 1 SCRUMPTIOUS 9-BY-12-INCH BAKING DISH

In my humble opinion, the trick to good mac and cheese is layering the cheese along with the sauce in the dish at least twice and making sure you have a texture change by adding a crisp bite or crunch to the top. So many chefs have variations, ranging from potato chips to bacon to Ritz crackers to nuts. My preference is adding buttered panko, evenly sprinkled across the top. It's all about what makes you happy!

Oh, and don't even think about using pre-shredded cheese. If you want to do this right, you have to use some elbow grease and just shred the cheese yourself. You can do it. Not only will you get a much better-tasting dish, but you will also skip those added invisibles that manufacturers often put in shredded products to keep them "fresh."

1 pound elbow or shell pasta

½ cup unsalted butter (at room temperature if you can)

½ cup all-purpose flour

1½ cups whole milk

2 cups heavy cream
I know… just do it!

Paprika, ground

Maldon sea salt flakes

Freshly ground black pepper

3½ cups freshly grated Gruyère
+ your elbow grease.

3½ cups freshly grated sharp, aged cheddar Seriously, you'd better be hand-grating all the cheese. Mix together Gruyère and cheddar.

1 cup panko breadcrumbs

2 ounces unsalted butter, melted

Mix together panko and butter at the end for the topper.

Preheat oven to 350°F. Butter a 9-by-12-inch baking dish (or whatever ovenproof dish you want to serve the mac and cheese in). Set aside.

On the stove, bring a large pot of salted water to a boil. Add the dried pasta and cook to al dente. *It's really important not to overcook the pasta, so watch this closely.*

In a sauté pan, melt the butter over medium heat. Add the flour to the butter and whisk to make a roux. Keep whisking for about 60 to 90 seconds, until well cooked through.

Slowly pour in the milk and then the cream, whisking continuously until thoroughly incorporated. Leave on the stove over medium-low heat to thicken, whisking occasionally, until it has a gravy-like consistency.

Remove from heat and season with paprika, Maldon salt, and black pepper to your taste. Add half the mixed cheese in small batches to the sauce, being careful to reserve the other half for layering in the dish. As you add the cheese to the sauce, mix thoroughly. Take your time with this.

In either the same pot or a large bowl, combine the drained pasta with the cheese sauce, stirring to fully incorporate. Pour half the pasta mixture into the prepared baking dish. Top with half the remaining cheese. Add the remaining pasta and cheese sauce mixture and sprinkle over with the remaining cheese.

Add the panko/butter mixture to the top by sprinkling evenly over the dish and bake for 15 to 20 minutes, or until bubbling. Finish for 1 to 2 minutes under the broiler to get a nice, even brown top. Serve hot.

There is no doubt that joy absolutely needs to guide your decisions too—and we'll dig into that in a later chapter—but at this stage of your career, you mostly want to pay attention to how you are feeling, what skills you want to learn, and what kind of experiences you want to gain. And if it hasn't become obvious to you by now, sometimes moving *forward* can mean making a side step to gain that experience and learn those skills. Maybe you love your job working the line in an airline catering facility because you adore the team you're working with, and then you find out there is an opening for an entry-level food safety ambassador and realize that food safety is more fascinating to you. The pay is the same and you'd have to leave your friends, but the role will offer a whole new world of skills to learn. If that's where your interest is pointing, make the leap and take the job, because it will be a badass investment in your long-term career. You'll become a more valuable worker because you'll gain more skills, and in the process, you'll learn more about what you love and what you don't. And those learnings will guide you toward whatever is next.

Sometimes, moving forward can even mean taking a step back, reassessing, and starting all over again in a new direction. *Yep, I did that.* During my work with the commodities broker, I kept returning to the fact that I loved food and people and connecting both through cooking and creating an environment around it all. So, I made a series of scary decisions—like that one I mentioned in chapter 1, when I left my steady job and flew to Paris to earn my degree in cuisine at Le Cordon Bleu. That was followed later by a brief culinary *stage* (internship) at the Plaza Athénée (that's the five-star hotel in Paris where Carrie breaks up with "The Russian" in *Sex and the City*, by the way), and then getting my first official chef job in London. All the while, I faced pointed criticism from some key members of my family, who thought I was crazy to leave a good-paying job in my mid-twenties to move to a foreign country and start making an hourly wage all over again. *More crumby jobs? By choice?* It made my decision-making all the more painful—I felt like I was disappointing those closest to me, as if I was dropping out of high school all over again. It really made me question myself. *There was a lot of churn.* But I wanted to try cooking professionally because I thought I would

love it and be really good at it. And if I failed? Well, you can't regret trying and failing. You can only regret never trying at all.

Being able to go to culinary school in Paris was a gift, a rare, precious opportunity I fully recognize most folks will not get, but there
are so many other opportunities you can seize to follow your passion—
local programs, scholarships, internships, even simply working in a
restaurant for a few months to see if you truly enjoy it. Culinary school
taught me how to cook. I was so fortunate to learn the techniques of
traditional French cooking from some incredible chefs, but it did not
teach me as much as experience later did. It's not like they taught me
a class on global menu development. Or how to staff a restaurant, create and fine-tune ideal operating budgets, or make sure my restaurant
didn't go bankrupt. That was all institutional knowledge passed on to
me over the years while I was doing each job as it came. I learned it all
by being brave enough to wade into the unknown.

So, let's skip forward after all that—after the agonizing over leaving
my job, after Le Cordon Bleu, after the internship in Paris and the later
work in London, and after my return to LA. Suddenly I'm being offered
an executive chef job at a fine dining restaurant in my hometown of Pasadena. My dream job! I would do the work I wanted to do and be able to
establish a stable life with a starting salary of almost $50,000—double
the pay I was receiving at the time. Hurray!

But—plot twist!—I quickly discovered that I did not actually enjoy
running a kitchen. The lifestyle was too challenging: I was working up
to sixteen hours a day, six days a week. I hadn't considered how the
hours of operation would upend my work-life balance. A leadership
role in a restaurant with a bar and high-volume brunches on weekends—oh, and it was also a favorite holiday meal spot—turned out to
be not a good path toward the stability I was craving. *Not so much with
the "hurray!" as it turns out.* I remember a particularly tough weekend
spent binning wine—that was when I got totally fed up. Have you ever
tried to reorganize a restaurant wine cellar? You have to pull and record
every bottle and match it to a coding number and create an iron-clad
inventory system so that bottles are super easy to find quickly when
ordered and also so they don't "walk away." I remember thinking that

there was no way this was worth so much time away from my friends and family.

It was deeply upsetting to have worked all those years and come all this way to get into my dream job and realize I hated it. *What the hell had I done?* I dove into the jobs section on Craigslist in search of a culinary job with regular business hours, but I had little hope such a thing even existed in the industry. As I scrolled through the listings, though, that hope rekindled. There were so many opportunities available: openings in bookkeeping, HR, graphic design, serving, hosting, stadiums, schools and universities; there were corporate management roles, jobs in photography, writing and editing, hotels, nightlife, packaging, retail—all connected to food. It might sound strange after everything I had already experienced, but I had never considered this broad range of opportunities before. And maybe you haven't, either.

I am sharing all of this with you because it's important for you to trust that, in this sea of choices, when you make a wrong move, it is simply part of a bigger story that can take you one step closer to the *right* move. When I left that restaurant in Pasadena, I was so sad to leave my incredible team—and so sad to leave menu favorites behind that felt like they had become a part of my edible soul (including my favorite cheeseburger in the world, which featured melty, lavish Gruyère and a perfectly grilled sourdough bun and was served with teeny-tiny parsleyed matchstick fries and homemade tomato compote . . . *sigh*). But by listening to my instincts and being willing to take risks, I managed to forge a "road less traveled" that took me closer and closer to what I love, all while bringing those hard-earned learnings with me. And now here we are, you and I, talking about building your dream career in the food world one step at a time, which right now feels like the perfect new turn in my long and winding career.

Sometimes the Obvious Is Hiding in Plain Sight

There is an underdiscussed truth about entry-level workers and what it takes to start moving "up the ladder." It goes like this: If you are able to demonstrate the basic, fundamental characteristics that lead to the successful execution of your daily job duties—and when I say "basic," I mean things like being on time, being reliable, and keeping your agreements—and if you are able to contribute positively to your work environment and avoid engaging in any "funny business," then you *will* get promoted if there are roles available to promote you into. And, of course, promotion = more moolah.

And if your employer is small, and there aren't obvious roles to move into, someone is going to want you somewhere else—you can absolutely count on it. There is such a shortage of people who consistently bring these core skills to the table that they are in hot demand *all* the time. These boots-on-the-ground roles are critically important to the overall success of any organization. And remember what I said before: Employers are not (yet!) doing enough to explain, highlight, and respectfully demonstrate the value of these jobs, even when they invest heavily in employee development. Which means somehow you have to magically understand this truth on your own. I sure didn't when I did these jobs.

We need to bridge this gap in understanding the power of these roles—like, now! The stories in this book will show you how to use these opportunities, and I am here to fiercely champion your success by helping you along your way. I want to open your eyes to just a few of the doorways that might be hiding in plain sight all around you and give you some strategies for knocking on them. So let's dig in.

Start by Digging Where You Stand

Whether or not you can advance in your current company depends a lot on what kind of pathways exist there. Take a survey of the mid-level roles you might be able to move up and into. Shift supervisor? Assistant manager? Manager? If there are other people in your company who are holding roles like these, then you can hold them, too.

If you work in a bigger company, your managers and leaders are constantly looking at their teams and "succession planning"—meaning, determining how they are going to fill roles when the people who have them now get promoted or leave the business. That means that the folks who consistently demonstrate those core skills I listed earlier are already quietly getting lined up for professional development and advancement, often without them even knowing. Recruiting and training new employees is very expensive and time-consuming for companies large and small, so executives and business owners are always making big investments in employee retention, which is a major factor in the overall health and success of any business. *The fact that this is probably never communicated to you is exactly that vast disconnect I have been referring to.*

In fact, employee retention is a constant consideration at every level of a business, and one of the key functions of a DEI & Talent team and managers in every sector of the industry; they are doing this behind closed doors all the time. Planning for the future, identifying key talent, and filling in any knowledge or skill gaps you may have are all an essential part of protecting the business, ensuring continuity, and preparing for expansion, and yet no one really talks about this at the entry level. But if you are an asset to your team, there is a very high probability that your boss—as well as your boss's boss, and sometimes even that boss's boss—will be having conversations about your performance and how they see your skills fitting in over the longer term.

This is especially applicable to brands in expanding markets, where they are opening locations as fast as they can and need experienced hourly workers to transfer over and help get things launched. You can't rapidly grow a business from six locations to sixty without relying heavily on the frontline team members who know how to get things done. Who do you think operates those new locations? Who do you think trains all those new employees? That's right: it's the folks who consistently brought their A-game and helped things run smoothly at the original locations.

So whether it's a bakery, coffee shop, or sandwich joint; whether it's sit-down, take-away, fast-casual, fast-food, grocery, catering, packaged food, or any other concept or operating model, the team members who know the brand and bring their whole selves to work are the ones who are going to find wild opportunities waiting for them. *Always.*

And if I can play "Professor Obvious" for a moment: the bigger the company, or the more rapidly it's expanding, the bigger the opportunities for wage increases and career advancement. Not just bigger, but sooner, too.

Say Yes to Opportunity

Half of the art of moving ahead is to walk through an open door when one is presented to you. For some reason, when offered opportunities that may not have a known outcome, many people's response is to just stroll right by the moment. I think that's nuts. My entire career has been built on saying yes to opportunities, *especially* when it wasn't clear exactly where that opportunity would lead.

Let me illustrate this with a singular moment that happened after I left that restaurant in Pasadena. I finally found a job that seemed like the perfect next step: overseeing the kitchen operations for an international café brand in the LA market. It was my first foray into multi-unit operational management (I didn't even know that existed!) and it was a steep learning curve, but I was all in and thrilled to work with such incredible people and learn yet another new side of the business. I was about nine months into the role when an executive (whom I will call "Le Gros Fromage") came into town from New York City to get a look at the operations and spend time with the team. We had a group dinner at a restaurant on the Westside, and I remember being so excited about having the chance to spend time with him and hear his views on the business. I couldn't believe my lucky stars when I was seated next to him! We had a pleasant chat during dinner, and he made a toast to the team's success. He gave us some encouraging feedback from his visits to our various locations around LA. The wine was flowing, folks were energized and happy, and it was a good moment amid our busy restaurant life.

At one point, "Le Gros Fromage" mentioned some challenges he was facing with parts of the European business. In one particular country, he had been trying to shape up the brand consistency and uniformity of the customer experience in the restaurants there, to better meet the expectations of what a visit there *should* look and feel like. Think of it like this: Imagine you get that "I'm starving" feeling and head to your local McDonald's. You've been going there your whole life, and what you order is the same as what you've always ordered. When it arrives, it looks the same, it's packaged the same, and it tastes the same. Same. Same. *Same.*

Now, imagine you went to a McDonald's in Spain expecting to find those same menu items and that same experience. But no! Wait! The menu offers only cold baguette sandwiches and sushi. Sushi? *WTF.* Now you're confused, pissed off, *and* starving. Well, something very much like that was happening overseas in some of the restaurants, and it sounded as if things had gotten a little off track.

As it turned out, "Le Gros Fromage" knew I had spent time living and working in Europe, and we had a chat about my experiences there and my grasp of the different languages and cultures. Suddenly, out of nowhere, he invited me to go back overseas for a three-month project to help the local leadership get the restaurants in better shape. I had been working for this business for *less than a year,* and over a glass of wine at a casual dinner, an offer to move overseas was put on the table. Just like that.

I couldn't believe it. I was stunned and *exploding* with happiness. Hell to the *yes!* In my most calm and professional voice, I agreed (I had to suppress my inner screaming so he wouldn't immediately regret his offer). The next day, when I told my direct boss what had happened, he laughed and said he knew about it and knew I would, of course, say yes. It turns out that the whole thing was a setup and he and "Le Gros Fromage" had already discussed the idea. Remember what I said about those behind-closed-doors conversations about your future?

Within a few weeks, I was on my way back to Europe to whip the teams, menus, and profits into good shape. I didn't know it at the time, but I would remain there for almost a year, and it launched my career in an entirely new direction of global travel and menu and operational oversight. Eventually, I became the director of food and beverage operations for the master franchise of a restaurant company that operated in nineteen countries with over 150 locations. *All because I said yes to an unexpected twelve-week project one night at dinner.*

I've seen this same scenario repeat so many times over the years for others who have jumped at opportunities rather than let them pass by. Once, at another international food brand, I put out an internal call for a temporary intern to join my food team and help with menu development and product launches. A young man who had been making sandwiches at one of our stores turned up for his interview in a crisp, sharp outfit, and, while nervous, he was clearly prepared. He had a passion for food, marketing, and custom tennis shoes, which he was trying to build into a small business on the side. He had gone to college, but he had struggled to find a job in his field, so he had taken an hourly wage job and was living in the Bronx with his mom.

I offered him the internship and was instantly impressed with his ability to navigate both the creative side of the work (making delicious recipes) and the business side (making those recipes profitable). Make no mistake—that combination of creative talent and business savvy is incredibly rare to find, and it matters a lot in menu development. He was also easy to work with, kept his agreements, and was completely coachable and willing to learn.

By saying yes to the opportunity, this young man eventually earned himself a full-time role on my team and went on to have a wonderful career in product development. Today, he's in leadership, overseeing R&D for a well-known food brand on the West Coast. From sandwich maker to R&D leader, and all it took was the willingness to step into the unknown and bring his best every day.

The hard truth about opportunities is that not many will arrive in one person's lifetime. And at some point, they simply stop showing up—especially if you're never willing to meet the moment. So, I challenge you to say yes when they come. Take the risk and see what happens. At the very least, you will learn valuable insights, make new relationships, and see things you otherwise wouldn't have seen. And always remember that moving forward can sometimes mean sideways and even backwards. Moving is motion, learning is growth, and paying attention to how you feel is the critical piece to carving your path and creating a career beyond your dreams.

TIME TO GET INTO MISE MODE

**Your prep for spotting—and grabbing—
all the opportunities you can
as you look for your next steps.**

MINDSET SHIFT: There is no single answer to your career questions, and you will learn from all of it. Experience is the greatest gift of all, and every part of your journey will end up being valuable to you in some way, even if you change direction a dozen times.

TRADE SECRET: Entry-level roles are powerful career-building vehicles. By saying yes to opportunities as they reveal themselves, you will gain much more experience—way faster. Experience = Promotions, and Promotions = Advancement, so grab those opportunities when they come.

LEADERSHIP LOWDOWN: If you work in a larger food company, your bosses are already talking about you and your potential future as a manager and beyond. Become that standout employee who truly brings their A-game, and they *will* take notice.

INSIDER DISH

Alert! Industry rock star sharing ALL the tips! This way!

4

FROM MISE TO PLATE

What It Really Takes to Get Ahead

The ways that your colleagues experience you will become your professional reputation— **and it will either fuel your ascent or keep you anchored.**

IT'S ONE THING to strategize your way from job to job, but it's another thing altogether to mold yourself into the kind of professional who has obvious leadership qualities, both in what you can do and in who you are. Yes, your resilience muscle will get you through the "crumby" jobs and into the better stuff. But it's the commitment in your mind and heart that will create the pathway to management and ultimately leadership, if that's what you want to achieve. As distant as those roles may seem, the work starts now, at the entry level.

Remember: You must never think that your background or circumstances can prevent you from reaching the executive level if that's what you want for yourself. Look at the president or CEO of your current company. Or, if you work for a small business like an independent restaurant or catering company, look at the owner. How did they get started? Do they have a degree in everything it takes to run a business—finance, architecture, engineering, recruiting, DEI & Talent team? Do they even have a culinary degree? Probably not. More likely, they have accumulated related experience over their career in various jobs and through working with people from all sorts of backgrounds and who possess distinctive skills. While senior leaders will have core expertise (and, yes, many do have degrees as well, sometimes acquired later in life, when they knew better what kind of certification they needed), they are absolutely not experts in everything. They know how to identify and rely on talented professionals, navigate difficult and complex situations, work well with others, and achieve the performance needed to lead their organizations successfully and drive fantastic results.

No one is born with these skills. Those leaders picked them up and fine-tuned them along the way, starting from when they were working in jobs much like the one you might hold now. So, here are a few of the lessons you need to start paying attention to if you want to gain the most possible value from your hourly wage years and set yourself up for the widest and highest possible range of opportunity down the road.

Relationships Matter—Like, a Lot

Are you a good coworker? Really, think about it: Would the people you work with now sign up to work with you again, wherever they land next? Here is a fact I wish someone had told me when I was younger: Maintaining positive relationships is about more than just making friends and having fun at work on a day-to-day basis (although that's all important, too). It is literally the key to success in your career. If you are easy to work with, reliable, and trustworthy, your colleagues will remember, and they will bring you along with them as they start to develop their own teams. It's a very real and important thing that happens—your personal relationships move you to other levels of your career all the time. *Colleagues today will become bosses tomorrow.*

I once had a colleague at an international brand who worked with me on the same franchise team. We had such a laugh while we tackled big, hairy projects all over the globe, and we always found a productive, easy work rhythm. He had a great business mind and always kept his agreements. Eventually, he moved on to become a VP at another food brand, and a few years later, he asked me to consult for him. I flew to Manhattan and he introduced me to the big boss, and quite unexpectedly I landed an offer to oversee the company's food and beverage platform. These kinds of opportunities arose several times in my career, and it has been the same for everyone I know in this industry. You could rack up all the college degrees in the world and the knowledge you acquired would never be as important as whether or not your coworkers are happy to see your name when the weekly shift schedule is posted. Once you get to the leadership level, I would go as far as to say that success is 75 percent relationships and 25 percent skill. Maybe even 85/15. No, I am not exaggerating. It's that important. This is my observation after two decades of management experience and also the result of quizzing individual executives over many meals. It's actually my favorite dinner party question for senior leaders, and I seriously wish someone had just told me this from the outset. *Personal relationships are the key to unlocking career success.* That's your ticket. Pass it on.

So, what if not everyone likes you? I mean, it's gonna happen sometimes. There is only one Tom Hanks in the world, and that's not you. At times, you're probably going to irritate or offend; your style might be too direct or not direct enough; you might move too quickly for some, too slowly for others; and you could really tick some people off. It's kind of like cilantro. Some people absolutely adore the fresh, distinctive experience it brings to a dish. Others detest it with a passion and think it tastes like moldy soap or even super-bad breath. They will even claim to be allergic just to ensure that not even a whiff of cilantro ever touches their plate. Why are we suddenly talking about cilantro? Because *you* are cilantro. *I* am cilantro. *Everyone* is cilantro... well, except maybe Tom Hanks. My point is, not everyone is going to like you, and you can't control that.

But you *can* control your actions and behavior. At the end of each day, you want to be proud of how you showed up for your team, colleagues, and leadership. Working well with others means minimizing the drama you bring to the workplace and refusing to amplify the drama brought in by others; it means having your colleagues and bosses experience you as trustworthy, hardworking, and reliable; and it means boosting the success of others and generally being a good colleague.

It also means picking your battles. Here's another unavoidable fact of life: not only will there be people who don't like you, but there will also be those you don't like, and situations you don't think are fair. Even when you're dead right about something, learning to keep your cool and take your losses in stride will set you apart from others. You don't need to be BFFs with every person you work with, but you do have to demonstrate your reliability in being a solid team player and find ways to authentically connect with and assist those around you. The ways in which your colleagues experience you will become your professional reputation—and it will either fuel your ascent or keep you anchored.

Did I Mention It's Not Always Fair?

Here's the thing: sometimes getting along can also mean "sucking it up." Let's face it, working relationships and company cultures can be tough and unpleasant. Toxic even. I spent *years* committing myself to maintaining an intentional, professional attitude at work—and what I sometimes got in response was crushing feedback like, "You need to smile more," or, "You need to loosen up." And that's what was said to my face. Some of the things *not* said to my face included the old classics like, "What a bitch," and "She needs to get laid!" I could deal with all of that (what woman in the workplace doesn't deal with crap like this at some point in her career?), but what I couldn't deal with was losing an opportunity because something I did outside of work got fed into the rumor mill and ended up costing me my credibility. So, I kept my private life totally separate from my professional life.

In retrospect, I probably went too far in that direction, and it took years to find a comfortable way to intertwine my personal and professional lives. But the fact is, if you behave in a way you would not want your mother to know about, *it will bite you in the ass*. I once worked with a young, super-talented manager who, on a night out with some colleagues, apparently got a little too drunk and a little too personal about what kind of piercings she had and where. On a different occasion, she allegedly made out with a married executive in public, and eventually all sorts of unsavory tales started to emerge in the daily office gossip. She was a very capable professional, but she blew her own credibility in the way she tried to connect with others outside of the office. People spoke ferociously about her behind her back and even started inviting her out and egging on the behavior to get more stories to giggle about. She was never promoted and ended up leaving the business with little to show from her time there.

Is any of this fair? No. Were the men who worked alongside that professional worried about losing opportunities because of how *they* acted at the bar? I hate saying this, but probably not. Even in my own case, despite the fact that I had good, solid relationships with my colleagues and was known for delivering consistent, high-quality, and profitable results, and even though I kept a cautious social distance from colleagues in my early management roles, I was still not able to escape some truly mind-blowing, career-altering dynamics, none of which were fair (another book, another time).

People are going to talk—sometimes because of your behavior, sometimes regardless of it. Just be intentional about what you put out there. I have a lovely uncle who always says, "Whatever someone thinks about you is none of your business"—meaning you shouldn't spend time or energy focused on other people's opinions because you can't control them. What you *can* control is your own behavior, so make sure you embody and demonstrate what you want others to see and talk about. In the long run, that will win out over gossip.

You Have to Learn to Serve

There's another aspect of workplace relationships in the food industry that isn't often thought of in those terms: your relationship with your customers. At the beginning of your career, you will likely deal with customer service every day—in fact, chances are you're dealing with it right now in your current job. It can be extremely rewarding to connect with people from all walks of life and to find ways to bring them joy. It can also feel like you've been covered in chum and thrown into a shark tank.

As you learn the ropes of your new job, you will most likely be in full view of customers. Everything you do will have an effect on their experience, from cleaning tables and bathrooms, to driving and delivering, to stocking the shelves, taking orders, and making cappuccinos. They're watching you and reacting to you all the time.

This is the theater. This is the experience. This is what people are paying for.

From the customer's view, they are entering your business to spend their money, and they want something good in return. *Of course,* they are going to have opinions and expectations about this experience. We all do! Whether it's their first time visiting or they're a regular, they are coming for the deliciousness and the service, and to be nurtured in the process. It's your job to give them what they are expecting.

Giving good service seems self-evident, but this is one of the hardest parts of the job when you start out. And it is also one of the most underrated ways to make your mark as you climb the ladder. If you start paying attention, you will see the gaps in customer service so clearly and you will find your own natural and authentic ways to respond to them. This effort will pay off because it's far more affordable to do whatever it takes to keep a customer than it is to try to win one back after you've lost them, and established businesses know this. (Google "customer acquisition and retention strategies" if you want to know more.) What this means is that smart bosses will reward you for taking the initiative to keep a customer from walking out the door forever.

Back when I was working at Pret A Manger, the team members were all brilliantly empowered to offer free food and drinks to customers. What this meant was that if someone complained that their skim milk latte had been accidentally made with soy milk, a team member could remake the drink *and* give a brownie or croissant to make up for the error. This policy made it easy to "connect and correct" on the spot— *fast*. But what about when it was the customer who was in the wrong?

Let me tell you one of those "scary stories" that anyone working in a customer-facing role will have in their back pocket, ready to share over drinks. I remember a particularly angry woman who didn't want to remove her small dog from her lap while she dined on the patio at a restaurant where I was working as a manager. Not only was this a violation of the local health code, but she also kept allowing her pet to lick her plate while she ate. Her server tried repeatedly to get her to put the dog down on the ground, but she absolutely refused and became more and more disruptive.

The server was very distressed, so I went and introduced myself as a manager. But before I could explain about the law, the customer started hurling abuse at me and complaining about being targeted. I knew I needed to stay calm and kind, so I listened and let her get it all out. It was awful and, frankly, humiliating. When she was finally finished, I told her that I heard her and was sorry she was upset, but she needed to understand that what she was doing was a health code violation, and that the restaurant would be fined and possibly closed if the health inspector came by. I also explained that the other customers couldn't possibly know the health status of the animal, and that everyone wants to eat in a place where they felt comfortable. In short, I gave her all the reasons her behavior was unacceptable. She calmed down and said she would rather leave than force her dog to be on the ground, and that other restaurants never seemed to mind (which I knew was a crock of you-know-what). I gave her my card and told her she was welcome back anytime with her dog if she wanted to follow the rules, and that I was happy to pick up her check so that she could leave immediately. She took the card, stood up, and walked out.

Let's be real. My blood pressure reached heart attack level during this exchange, but I didn't show it—I just stayed outwardly calm and put my focus on being a good example for my team while holding my ground. What I really wanted to say was this: *Lady, are you fucking kidding me?? Just put your dog on the floor, because this is revolting, and no one would be cool with this. Actual humans eat off these plates. Get out,* (and then in the voice of the Wicked Witch in *The Wizard of Oz*), *and your little dog, too!* But instead, I exercised my resilience muscle. Talk about sitting with discomfort. Sheesh.

Here's the thing: I knew my team was watching how this situation was being handled, and I wanted to be a good example, show empathy, and also not be a doormat. In fact, in training sessions for new employees, I used to tell a story for team members to lean on during the inevitable and difficult moments they would face being in service. The stories would change a bit here and there, but the gist was this: Pretend for a moment that *you* are an angry customer. Your credit is maxed, you're on your last $20, and you're on the way to an interview for a job you are desperate to win. Before you left the house, you realized your cat hair-balled all over the nicely laid-out outfit you spent hours stressing about the night before, and you had to scramble to plan B. On your way to the interview, you realize you left your phone at home. Then the bus doesn't come and you can't call an Uber because . . . no phone! You see a café up the street and decide to spend your last dollars on a cappuccino and chocolate chip cookie while you figure out how the heck you are going to pay your bills and try to convince your potential employer that you didn't skip the interview but had an unavoidable travel glitch. You are so upset, and you just know that at least for this moment, you are going to feel normal and successful by having a cappuccino and *goddamn chocolate chip cookie* like everyone else—and when your drink arrives, it is *green*. WTF. And the cookie is oatmeal raisin. You were looking forward to *one small thing* in a life that feels like it's going down in flames, and when it shows up, it's *wrong*. So you lose your mind and unleash holy hell on the server.

Now, flip the story. Imagine that you are the server, and this hot mess of a person is screaming at you because of a matcha latte and a cookie, and it's gone nuclear. How do you fix this problem quickly and stay calm through it all? You remember that it's never about you, or even about your mistake. It may not be possible to know about all the stuff that happened before you gave them the wrong drink and the wrong cookie, but it is always possible to remember that everyone is going through their own battles, and most of the time, the way they are behaving is related to that and not to whatever small situation is at hand. Bottom line: You can't know what another person is experiencing, but you can choose to be kind. And then you can move on.

Learning to serve and solve problems in this way takes a lot of patience, practice, and emotional maturity. But I want to tell you, when you correct something and make it right, and when your customer is satisfied and smiling and feels heard and respected, it feels *so good*. Customer service is one unique area of the food industry that provides the opportunity to deal with people and their emotions, to become a part of their story for the day, to make a personal impact through your own actions and behaviors. This is what I love so much about this side of the industry—we are nourishing not just people's bodies but also their *souls*. It's so cool and such a privilege to be able to do that for a living— and always being aware of how you are using that power and privilege will have a massive effect on where your career goes, and how much it fulfills you as you get there.

JFDI as a Superpower

It's not just customers who are going to seem unreasonable over the course of your early career. You are going to experience times when your boss has to communicate something to you urgently, and you will be asked to act right then and there. *Immediately.* They're not going to have time to explain what's going on or why it needs to be done, but you're going to have to do it, and fast. This is commonly referred to in the food world as a JFDI, or "Just Fucking Do It." Good managers won't abuse these moments or make every task a "just do it now and ask me why later" moment. But as an employee, you are not going to be able escape these very necessary and often poorly timed requests. We all experience them in this industry, at almost every level of our careers—and in the food world, every second counts.

And when JFDIs arrive? *Just do it. Really.*

One of my all-time favorite JFDI moments happened in a very busy, high-volume corporate restaurant operation, when I got word from my boss that one of the company directors was unhappy that there was no Diet Coke in his office pantry. I was in the middle of a serious, high-priority DEI & Talent team meeting discussing personnel issues when I got the text: "Big Cheese is pissed off he can't find a Diet Coke." My immediate reaction was to think, "C'mon—this entire building is littered with refrigerators stocked with every beverage you can imagine. Use your legs, man!" But then the next text arrived: "Big Cheese wants you to bring a Diet Coke to his meeting room STAT."

I knew at that moment it was a JFDI, and I had been around long enough to know when not to push back, no matter what other business I had going on. So I did it. At that point in my career, I was leading a team of a thousand people on the ground and another several hundred remotely. I was the Big Cheese of my own area of the business, and I knew after all the years in my career that things can often seem obnoxious, frivolous, or flat-out wrong—like, say, when you're in a senior position but an executive makes you their errand girl—but you have to be strategic and put your career before your personal feelings. Complain with your trusted friends over a glass of wine later. (I sure did.) Ask your immediate boss about the "why" later. But JFDI now.

"Lose Your Mind" Chocolate Chip Cookies

ALL IN TAKES ABOUT 30 TO 40 MINUTES • ACTIVE TIME 20 MINUTES

MAKES 25 TO 40+ COOKIES, DEPENDING ON HOW BIG YOU LIKE THEM

I like them small!

Whenever I make a batch of these cookies, I freeze half the dough in plastic wrap in the shape of a log. That way I have at-the-ready cookies on hand at all times!

1½ cups unsalted butter, melted and left to rest

1¾ cups light brown sugar, softened

4½ cups all-purpose flour

1 teaspoon baking soda

2 whole eggs

2 additional egg yolks

4 teaspoons vanilla extract

2¾ cups milk chocolate chips
Callebaut is my fave, but any milk chocolate chip should work well.

Optional: Maldon sea salt to sprinkle on top once baked
I really prefer them this way. Salt = heaven.

Preheat oven to 325°F. Melt the butter and set aside.

Add light brown sugar to a stand mixer and give it a good mix with the paddle attachment to get all the lumps out. In a separate bowl, add the baking soda and flour and put once through a flour sifter if you have one. Once sifted, use a whisk to fully mix the baking soda and flour so it is evenly distributed. Set aside.

Add the melted butter to the brown sugar and mix until soft and fully incorporated. Slowly add in the vanilla and eggs, including the additional yolks, and mix until just incorporated.

Add the flour/baking soda mixture slowly and stop mixing as soon as it is all together. Don't overmix! Add the chocolate chips and gently fold them into the dough with a spatula to evenly distribute. *This is the moment when you can separate the dough and freeze some if you want!*

On a baking sheet lined with parchment paper or a Silpat, drop the dough by rounded tablespoons or a cookie scoop and lightly press down on each cookie to hold it in place. Keep a small distance between them so they retain their gorgeous shape.

Bake for about 10 minutes for small cookies and up to 15 minutes for larger ones. You will know they are done when there is just the slightest brown edge forming on the bottom—they will still look pale and not really golden, so you might doubt they are ready, but they will be! Double-check with a toothpick to see if it comes out clean once inserted. These are easy to overbake, so stay focused! *Add your Maldon salt here if you like... highly recommended!*

Place cookies on a baking rack to cool, then enjoy.

Put this in your back pocket for when you are in charge: As much as you have to accept JFDIs as a junior team member, when you're a manager leading a team, there will be times when you need to employ them. Here's a tip from me to future-manager you: *Inform* your team up front about the likelihood of JFDIs so they know how to recognize them when one comes their way. "If you ever hear me say 'JFDI,' it's time for action. I promise I will circle back and give you the reason as soon as I can." Your team will appreciate the heads-up, you will share a laugh together, and they will fully show up for you in those trickier, time-sensitive moments.

Discover the Gift of Critical, Hard-to-Hear Feedback

There is one final skill you'll need if you want to move ahead in the food world, and that's to admit that you don't know everything, and that your way isn't necessarily always the best way. We all have the tendency to switch to autopilot and stop thinking through what we're doing or how we're doing it—we just *do it*. But as you move up the ladder, how you collaborate with others will be critical to achieving business goals, and for the overall success and career advancement of everyone you work with—especially your own. And your bosses and colleagues are all going to have opinions about how you show up and do your job, and especially how you could do it differently and better. So now is the time to start learning how to be vulnerable, how to admit that you don't know *every damn thing*, and how to turn feedback into the precious gift that it is. Think of it this way—it's information. Information is knowledge. *Knowledge is power.*

I remember so fondly the colleagues, leaders, and mentors who invested in my success, and in me personally, during my early career years. They listened to my concerns and issues with remarkable patience and had buckets of time and energy for finding solutions to all sorts of challenging scenarios. Even when they were kicking my ass and showing me how wrong I was (which was often!), I still came out of the experience feeling energized and inspired to work even harder.

They showed me how to think more productively and critically, and they not only gave me new tools but also showed me how to use them. Most importantly, they did all of this not by *telling* me what to do, but by *collaborating* with me and showing me enormous respect while guiding me toward positive results. It was a really enjoyable win-win.

The bad, ineffective managers I had, on the other hand, used critical feedback almost as a weapon—a way to demoralize, criticize, and demean their team's performance and skills without providing tools, genuine support, or solutions. Looking back on those early years, I can see that those particular folks had some serious emotional maturity issues—but truthfully, so did I in my own way. I was learning and growing up... we all were. I know, however, that I was better able to hear and process hard, challenging feedback from people who I felt were genuinely invested in my success and not just looking to personally criticize me.

Unfortunately, we can't pick our bosses, so if this happens to be your current scene, know that you're not alone and take heart. It will eventually change—it always does—and you will learn from all of it. Especially how to bring your game face in tough moments. (Which, incidentally, will also serve you later on in your career, too!)

From a career development standpoint, your managers are going to be watching to see if you are coachable, curious to learn, and able to take critical feedback in stride. They are also going to be assessing your ability to work effectively with the team and what your personal contribution is to the energy, environment, and, ultimately, performance outcomes. "Teamwork is the dream work" and "there is no 'I' in team," and all the other cheesy but ultimately accurate slogans that stress the importance of working together exist for a reason. Because we are stronger and better *together.* There is no such thing as a successful lone wolf in business.

Investing in a collaborative approach from the start and learning to take and value feedback—especially hard, tough, and negative feedback, and even more especially feedback you don't agree with—and then to turn it all into the information you need to work more effectively with those around you: this is a skill and a life lesson that will carry you forward to all the next levels of your career path.

TIME TO GET INTO MISE MODE

Your prep for gathering the skills, capabilities, and attitudes that will help you thrive in your career.

MINDSET SHIFT: You can't control how other people behave, and your job isn't always going to be fair. Tapping into empathy *and* your resilience muscle can help you keep your own emotions in check in the trickier moments.

TRADE SECRET: This is a fast-paced, unpredictable industry, and JFDIs are going to happen sometimes. Learn to recognize when it's time to keep your mouth shut and just *do*. You can always ask "why" and "what the heck" later.

LEADERSHIP LOWDOWN: As strange as it may seem, the relationships you develop and the way people experience you will have a much bigger impact on your career than your skills or knowledge. As you move up, your colleagues are moving up, too, so be a person they will remember as an asset.

INSIDER DISH

Ready for more career insights? You know what to do!

5

FIRE, KNIVES, AND FOOLERY

It's Time to Get Serious About Safety and Respect in the Workplace

What we do as food-industry professionals matters in the most significant ways you can imagine. **Human life and human health are in our hands.**

PICTURE A TYPICAL DAY in the life of a food-industry professional as you imagine it would be. What flashes across your mind? Are you envisioning a chill, relaxing picnic in the middle of your favorite park with whistling wind and birds chirping softly as you crack open a Mason jar of Grandma's Picnic Punch while tucking into a platter of perfectly seasoned fried chicken with your colleagues?

Probably not.

More likely, you are imagining a busy kitchen with dishes clattering and fires sparking in the background, and maybe a chef screaming, "Fire!" or "Pick up—table five!" Or perhaps you see a more industrial image, like a farm operation or a slaughterhouse with a crush of large animals and tons of heavy equipment. Whatever you envision, it probably reflects your inner understanding that the food world, while responsible for so many of the most joyful and delicious moments in our lives, is also responsible for some of most dangerous and deadly moments in the working world. Between endless opportunities for real, catastrophic physical injury, foodborne illnesses affecting both staff and customers, and even some hard-core bullying that is still rampant in certain areas of the industry, the food world has a truly dark side. *Yes, it's a painful truth, but we need to talk about it in order to set you up for success.*

Let's put all my resilience talk aside for a moment because, really, sometimes things happen that aren't the kind you can just tough out. Ever heard the saying "If you can't take the heat, get out of the kitchen"? Well, it's also important to be able to recognize when the problem really does lie in the heat and not in your ability to tolerate it, and to know what to do when that happens. Your resilience muscle will not save you from second-degree burns when you drop the roast beef you are searing with bare hands into the roasting pan and the grease suddenly splashes out from the melted fat cap. (Yep, that happened to reckless, shortcutting, younger chef me, and my hands were rendered useless for almost a month.)

You are going to face some incredibly tough, challenging, obnoxious, and even deadly moments in this business as you climb the ladder. There is just no way around it. And it's not all about physical danger either—it's also about the decisions you will have to make when you are confronted with toxic bosses and work environments. So, let's lay out some ways that you, personally, can make a difference in keeping your colleagues, customers, and yourself safe while also positively contributing to the culture of your work environment.

Surprise! You Don't Have to Be a Jerk to Run a Kitchen

Earlier in this book, we talked about the "crumby" jobs you're going to experience—work that's tedious, low-paying, exhausting, and even sometimes gross. But you might also experience a few moments or even entire workdays that go beyond "crumby" and into, well, flat-out horrifying. So, here's a question for you: How inspired would you be to continue in a job if your boss did something like scream at you at the top of his lungs in front of all of your colleagues, hold your head in between two pieces of bread, and yell, "WHAAAT ARE YOUUU?" until you gave the answer that he wanted ("An . . . an . . . idiot saaandwiiich?")? Maybe you wouldn't be too excited about going to work anymore, and maybe it would be a bit more challenging to be open about mistakes you've made along the way, due to the justifiable fear of the humiliating dressing down you might receive for being a normal, imperfect human.

And while that famous "idiot sandwich" scene is not actually real— it's from a parody video courtesy of chef Gordon Ramsay, Julie Chen, and James Corden—it's easy to believe it *is*, given the kind of "world-class asshole" behavior that talented, well-respected, and even famous chefs and business leaders across the industry used to be able to get away with.

And let me tell you, while the world has evolved and the food industry has finally started to say "nope!" to this kind of destructive conduct, it was experiencing behaviors very similar to that parody clip that informed future-leader me while I was climbing the ladder. My experiences in the kitchens of Paris and London were incredibly challenging, stressful, and even extremely demoralizing at times. I had never before been the target of such nasty, obnoxious behavior in my life. At the time, I couldn't understand why this was happening. Apparently, I rubbed up against all the norms in European kitchens: I was a woman. I was American. *Who the hell was I and why was I there?*

It all made me an easy target, and there was a lot of juvenile, unprofessional, and straight-up abusive behavior pointed at me. Between dodging airborne frying pans, being screamed at for not working fast enough, and having to navigate around chefs who were dry-humping their stoves throughout the day, it was an intense period in my career. Being at the very bottom of "the ladder," I was given all of the most obnoxious tasks, while the other chefs would laugh and "stop by" just to nag, mock, and harass me. And, yes, a lot of it was done intentionally, to try to make me quit. I still remember the super-fun tasks they gave me as part of that campaign . . . like boiling and peeling a thousand quail eggs with the demand that it be done in four hours—a time frame that is literally impossible. You have to boil them in batches in order to ensure they are cooked and cooled correctly. And have you ever tried to peel even a single quail egg? They are so fragile and teeny—it's hard not to create dents or take out chunks of egg. And you can't just *peel* them—you have to make sure they are perfect in every way. *That's the job.* After about fifty eggs, your fingers get all soft and wrinkly, and then they get cold, bitterly cold, because you are plunging them into ice water every few seconds. Then they go numb and you can't feel them or make them work properly anymore. And you still have nine hundred to go. *Total nightmare.*

I never understood why this kind of bullying behavior was celebrated or even allowed, because I saw it impact the performance of so many people. It burned people out, and I watched many chefs and other talented folks leave the industry because of it. The attitude was kind of like, "Well, I had to endure it, so now you have to." *What kind of garbage is that?* Somehow, I found the strength to stay. I leaned *hard* into my purpose for being there. I was there to learn, and I was not going to let those asshats knock me out of the game.

Here's a surprising truth. If I had the choice, I wouldn't skip over all that or delete those experiences from my work history. Sure, it would have been great to design a working environment that was support- ive, kind, nurturing and as "perfect in every way" as the quail eggs I had to prepare. But the fact is that without all of that confusion, pres- sure, and heartache, I don't think I would have had the opportunity to determine, let alone declare, what was important to me as a leader, or to realize that I wanted to strive to be a force for positive change and respect in the workplace. *You can absolutely demand the highest of stan- dards as a leader without engaging in taunting jackassery. Just sayin'.* Sometimes you have to "go through something" to realize what your val- ues are, and where your boundaries are. (You are going to hear this again and again throughout these pages—it's not an echo, it's just me nor- malizing how important and valuable the tough stuff is.) Being pushed far outside of your comfort zone is unfortunately a really good way to figure that out.

Commit to *Your* Values
(Even When Others Don't Seem to Have Any)

Why am I telling you all this? Because I want to be clear that it's not just in your "crumby" job era that you are going to meet these kinds of social and cultural challenges—in fact, such things often get harder and more complex as you climb the ladder because there is *way* more at stake, personally and professionally. Think: "My boss is a narcissistic micromanager, but I have a mortgage to pay and kids to feed. So, what do I do?"

Some of the people you will encounter as your career progresses are going to behave in more heinous and diabolical ways than you ever thought possible. This is not exclusive to the food industry—sadly, dirty games and politics seem to be inevitable in every corner of our professional universe, and professional adults, even the most senior and experienced leaders, do not always act fairly. But honestly? This is just life. I mean, is there anywhere you can fully avoid challenging personalities or moments? You can't even escape this at home! (You should just see my family with a Monopoly board. Ruthless doesn't even begin to cover it.) So, why do we all think there is going to be some fairy godmother who comes into our lives, waves a wand, and gives us a job with zero challenges and lots of money and all the things that supposedly make life easier? It just doesn't work like that. Not here, not anywhere.

In the beginning, as an entry-level cook, wanting to become an executive chef was more important to me than a comfortable work environment. So, I stayed in it. *Resilience muscle, baby.* Let's be real: All earned things in life require patience and grit. And in the food world that means working with challenging people in often unpleasant and dangerous conditions, being patient and strategic in the midst of it all, and not letting them get in your way.

I handled the challenges as best as I could, and I chose to take those moments as lessons and use them to make myself a better, more empathetic leader when I came into senior roles. I know you might have chosen *not* to tolerate the stove-humpers and bullying chefs, and that's okay. You know where the line is for yourself, you know what you want to achieve, and you should trust yourself to make the right decision *for your benefit*. It's up to you to monitor that line and decide when a situation is a survivable case of "jerks being jerks" and when the behavior of a boss or coworker has stepped over the line into abuse.

If you are faced with toxic behavior, think about where it's coming from: Is this one or two people or is this a reflection of the values of the organization? How do the most senior leaders treat others, especially those in the least powerful positions? Things are changing and, thanks in part to the impact of #MeToo, if the overall culture of a company is healthy, those behaving truly badly will likely not be in their roles for long. So, determine what's best for your career outcome and hold that as primary. It can be the fuel you need to make it through the tough experiences.

"...I Will Not Quit" *Asshats!*
...viled Quail Eggs

ALL IN TAKES ABOUT 20 MINUTES • ACTIVE TIME 15 MINUTES
MAKES 16 DEVILED EGGS

For me, 16 quail eggs is 1 portion, but for you, this recipe might offer small bites for 4 to 6 people. It also makes a great addition to a plate as a clever garnish.

---

1 tablespoon salt (sea salt preferred, but any old salt will do) *The salt is just for the boiling water.*

8 quail eggs

2 teaspoons mayonnaise

1 teaspoon Dijon mustard

Maldon sea salt flakes

Fresh black pepper

Paprika, ground

Chives, washed and dried and cut into 32¾-inch pieces

Optional: Thin-cut bacon strips, cooked and finely chopped into warm bacon bits

---

Hey! Read all the instructions all the way through before you start doing anything!

Boil some water in a small saucepot and add the "any old" salt. *Heavily salted water makes the eggs way easier to peel.*

Prepare a small ice bath from 75 percent ice and 25 percent cold water so you can immediately place the cooked eggs into the cooling bath. *If you don't have ice, no problem. Just run cold water over the eggs after boiling until they are fully submerged and cooled—takes a minute or two. The point is to stop them from overcooking.*

With a spoon, add eggs gently to the boiling water. Make sure the water is at a low simmer once they are all in.

Boil for 4 minutes, then remove the pot from the heat. Take out 1 egg with a slotted spoon and crack it open immediately to ensure it is hard-boiled before you remove the others. (The temperature the

eggs started at can impact cooking time—super-cold eggs usually cook well at 4 minutes, but if they were at room temperature already, try 3 minutes.)

Once hard-boiled, plunge the eggs into your ice bath to stop the cooking. When cooled, peel the quail eggs by gently hitting one side against the sink basin to form a crack and then taking your fingers to gently squish it all over and loosen the shell.

Using a straight-edged knife, cut the peeled eggs in half lengthwise and scoop the yolks into a small bowl using a tiny spoon or whatever you have that works.

To the yolks, add the Dijon mustard, mayonnaise, Maldon salt, a couple turns of black pepper, and a sprinkle of paprika. Mix well with a fork—it should be creamy.

Taste the mixture and adjust the seasoning to your preferences. Keep in mind that the bacon, if you're adding it, is salty.

If you want to be all cheffy about it, you can add the yolk mixture to a piping bag with a star tip and pipe little rosettes back into the egg whites. Or you can just spoon the yolk back in, which looks gorgeous and rustic.

Finish by sprinkling with paprika and another touch of Maldon. Place 2 chive sticks into the yolks in a slight crisscross shape (and add the bacon here if you like), and they are ready to eat!

If you do decide that the values of your current organization are not a good fit, it's time to consider your options. Start looking for an organization with leadership that demonstrates the kind of behavior and values you want to experience and embody. But! *Please* be strategic about when you quit. You have to think about your résumé overall and what it looks like when you move around too much. If it looks like you can't stay in any given role for more than three or four months or you have a lot of gaps, it can be a red flag. *Trust me on this one—I'm the one hiring.* So, use your resilience muscle and make sure you have your next job lined up before you quit. Then, once you do, walk out the door and look back only as a cautionary lesson.

Sometimes the Asshole Isn't Who You Think It Is

It also needs to be said that there is a *big* difference between a toxic culture and a demanding culture. Demanding cultures are typically found in high-stakes, high-growth environments where your whole team's talents will be stretched to achieve things never attempted before. That doesn't mean it's *bad*—that just means it's *challenging*. Learning how to solve problems like feeding an extra thousand people in a two-hour lunch window or successfully overseeing a newly acquired food truck operation when all of your experience and skills are in convenience store operations is part of maintaining a flexible "solutions" mindset. And you will need that mindset to meet critical moments again and again in your career.

I clearly remember one very capable manager who had valuable experience in restaurant operations: he was skilled with engaging his team and always produced strong results (a talent in itself). But when he was asked to pivot his day-to-day focus temporarily to step up to the sudden business need to provide off-site catering, the bitching and complaining he responded with was so mighty that he ended up poisoning the work environment for everyone. Within this high-performance, high-stakes business culture, the environment around this one manager became such a cesspool of negativity that it deeply impacted the entire team and, eventually, the overall performance of his department. He thought it was his *bosses* who were the assholes. Everyone around him thought something else.

I mean, sure, it can feel incredibly stressful when you're asked to do something outside of your job description, and it's easy to confuse that feeling with "my boss is an unreasonable fill-in-the-blank and I didn't sign up for this." So, let me put it this way: anytime I hear "that's not my job" come out of a team members' mouth, it creates an automatic ding on how I view their capacity to be nimble, productive, and positive. In the case of that particular manager, his bad 'tude and inability to make the mental U-turn required to meet the business moment lost him a ton of support within leadership. Eventually, he left the business, and that was a real shame because he could have been a real asset and gone very far in that organization. *Mindset really does matter.*

I'm telling you all of this because you are absolutely going to come across challenging bosses and demanding cultures and difficult projects and unexpected asks, and all are going to push you far past your current abilities. In some moments, it's not going to feel good. But it is *so, so* important to be able to distinguish that challenge from the abuse, toxicity, and *actual danger* you should definitely walk away from, because many of those challenging experiences will turn out to be some of the most valuable moments in your career. *Really.* It's *good* challenge, and I would hate to see you walk away from it all because you mistook it for something else. You are going to learn so much from those who stretch you past your current capabilities and experience, and from those who empower you to solve problems you have never solved for before. So, embrace it. Learn from it—all the good, bad, and ugly. Most importantly, don't let difficult people or hard moments knock you out of the ring. It's all up to you and how you choose to see the moment. My counsel to you? Take the learnings, make them into opportunities to shine, and lean on your resilience muscle to make it through.

"I'm Gonna Die for a Damn Sandwich"

Aside from the pressures and realities of toxic bullies and work environments, there are also endless ways to harm your customers, colleagues, and yourself in the industry. And that goes beyond the obvious illness, fire, and knives: The dangers in the food world also lurk in operating equipment, slips, trips, falls, repetitive movements, noise, and even work-related travel—anything that includes a way you or your colleagues could be at risk when performing your duties. That means that safety—*physical* safety—should be at the top of your mind and woven into every action you take in your working day. Your individual actions and decisions can do colossal, irreversible harm, both physically and emotionally, to yourself or others in this field of work. *This just cannot be understated.* The harsh reality is that many people have needlessly lost their lives or livelihoods due to totally avoidable incidents in the storage, handling, preparation, or enjoyment of food.

This is one of those topics where solemn, sober contemplation and focus is necessary. The programs and strategies around safety can and should be fun and engaging, but the core principle of the matter is that safety is a truly life-altering topic and deserves your respect and full attention at all times.

I personally have had several close calls with serious injury. One time, while cooking during an evening service, I had a piece of fish (a skate wing, to be specific) "explode" in my face when it hit a piping hot sauté pan full of clarified butter and oil. The searing pain is something that I still cannot describe in words and will never, ever forget—that exact moment when the hot liquid hit my actual eyeball. *Unbearable, instantaneous pain.* The explosion burned my cornea and caused splatter burns all around my face and eyes.

But here's the weird thing: as my team stepped in to take over the station, I couldn't shake the sense that I had let them down for not being able to carry on. I mean, we were, after all, people who used Super Glue to quick-close messy knife wounds so that we could carry on throughout service time without getting blood all over the food or plates. I felt ashamed and even humiliated that I couldn't keep cooking. I was also in a foreign country and didn't know where to go, so I walked feverishly to the subway station, keeping my head down so that no one would see the horror show of my face while I tried to figure out what to actually do about the injury. Thankfully, my then boyfriend met me at home and took me to a hospital, where I had my eye medically flushed out and got an appointment for the next morning at a specialized eye clinic. That accident stayed with me for a long time because it could have been so much worse—I was the luckiest of lucky on that day.

And that's just my own experience. Small children have lost their parents because of poorly managed food operations. Parents have lost their children because a food seller they trusted used unsafe cooking and handling practices. Does that feel heavy? It should because *it is*. What we do as food-industry professionals matters in the most significant ways you can imagine. Human life and human health are in our hands. *This is a sacred responsibility and a privilege that must not be squandered.*

So how does your personal contribution to the safety of yourself and others look? It looks like:

- paying attention to your training and to all the proper food handling and allergen control procedures;

- *using—really using—*all the gear and tools that should be well in place in any working environment to ensure optimal and safe conditions, such as goggles, masks, ear plugs, protective gloves, hard hats, harnesses—all of it; and

- speaking up and demanding these tools for yourself and your colleagues if they aren't in place.

Trust me when I say that these training programs and policies are not designed to waste your time, check boxes, or simply annoy you. They are designed to keep everyone safe. If you have questions about something, don't be shy: *ask.* You might be surprised by the reason that something is a certain way.

Take cold rooms, for example. The number of times I have heard complaints about them from people over the years is uncountable.

These production-line spaces hold prepared food and ingredients at a safe temperature (read: 41°F), which allows companies to safely optimize the usable shelf life of products like airline food or the sandwiches you mindlessly grab at the gas station. They're also *freakin' cold* to work in. If you're on one of those floors and you're too cold, that doesn't mean the room should be warmer (hello, food poisoning!); it means your leadership should be providing you with better personal gear to keep you warm and comfortable as you work. (This is something to remember when you are a leader and your team is complaining about safety procedures. *Solve the problem and keep your team comfortably able to function in refrigerated temperatures.*)

And remember when I said that even work-related *travel* can be dangerous? For many, a career in the food industry can involve a lot of travel. It certainly did for me, and while on my way to hundreds (if not thousands) of supplier meetings, conferences, site visits, and kitchen visits, the number of times "I'm gonna die for a damn sandwich" flashed through my mind is infinite. Sometimes it was simple airplane turbulence; sometimes it was a regional leader barreling us down the Autobahn in his station wagon so fast I thought I was going to have a heart attack and die. And I still chose risking death over speaking up to a superior! *Please* don't be young-manager me: if someone is putting you in a state of terror, speak up.

But sometimes, that feeling of danger can come right out of left field—like when I was in Moscow (in that golden sanction-free era post-Cold War and before the 2022 invasion of Ukraine) and a senior executive stuck his hand out on the side of the road and flagged down some random person's car. Not a cab, not a minibus, but just a total random stranger in a personal vehicle. The exec opened the door, muttered a few words in Russian, and just jumped in. I froze. *What was happening?* Were we actually getting into this unmarked, unknown vehicle with a stranger in the middle of Moscow? *Really?* As you can guess, I ultimately followed along because I didn't feel comfortable telling a senior executive that absolutely no f'ing way was I getting in a stranger's car and risking my life for a damn sandwich.

And if dumbass "cars-that-aren't-taxis" experiences like this don't seem dangerous enough, try sketchy "getting-dropped-at-crashpads-that-aren't-hotels" incidents, like the one time I was driven to a random apartment that was clearly *not a hotel* (and not an Airbnb, because those didn't exist) in a foreign country upon arrival in the middle of the night and just dumped there without much explanation (due to the language barrier). The local leadership had organized a driver (who was hours late) to collect me at the airport, and he simply pulled up to an apartment building—*not a hotel!*—grabbed my bags, opened the door, led me into a bedroom, pointed to a couple of cordless phones on a dresser, and said in broken English, "Phone will ring." No, I am not joking—this actually happened. And you can bet your ass I thought, *I am going to die for a sandwich.*

Thankfully, it's been a long time since I've had to worry about dying for a damn sandwich, but I know that if one of these incidents happened now, I'd speak up and advocate for my own safety. I hope you will learn from my mistakes and speak up the next time you feel unsafe at work.

Your personal contribution to the safety and culture of your workplace matters enormously. It's such a significant part of your work, and it's an area in which you can truly stand out and shine. Never underestimate the power you have in your hands to impact another human's life experience—*hold it all with the tenderest of care*—and, above all, to commit to bringing your best in every moment. That doesn't mean perfection, by the way; it means an intentional, mindful dedication to ask yourself in all the hard moments: Am I bringing my best? Am I doing my best? And then deliver your best in every way you can. *Safety first. Always.*

TIME TO GET INTO MISE MODE

Your prep for surviving and thriving in a sometimes raucous, sometimes risky, always dangerous industry.

MINDSET SHIFT: Things change fast in the food world, and you're going to be called on to do challenging things that are outside of your job description. When it happens, it can be a gift. Stay open-minded and never be afraid to pivot.

TRADE SECRET: Food and operational safety policies are never there just to be annoying. Each of us in the industry has a responsibility to take care of each other and the people we feed above and beyond anything else. It starts with you. Safety first—always.

LEADERSHIP LOWDOWN: Don't let one nasty team member or bad boss knock you out of the game. Resilience muscle, baby! Look at the bigger organizational structure and the values of the overall brand to decide if this is a place where you can grow into the kind of leader you want to be.

INSIDER DISH

You definitely don't want to miss out on these insights!

6

HAPPINESS IS A MAIN COURSE, NOT A SIDE DISH

Why Joy Is the Secret Ingredient You Need to Unlock the Career of Your Dreams

All of the clues you need
to direct your career
are already inside you.

NOW THAT WE'VE COVERED some of the harsher and more uncomfortable realities of working in the industry, it's time to talk about joy.
As cheesy as it sounds, joy—delight, happiness, glee, even!—matters
significantly in your life journey, don't you think? I mean, when you
consider that you spend most of the waking hours of your life working,
joy matters a whole heck of a lot in a job. So, focusing on what makes
you feel joyful is critical in helping you shape your career toward peak
life satisfaction.

When you close your eyes and think about the moments in life
that make you happiest, what do you see? If you pay attention to your
moods, reactions, feelings, and all the other clues that rest in your heart,
you can use those instincts to navigate your way in this industry to a
place that truly ignites those individual joys and passions. Do you love
gathering with friends, meeting new people, or hosting big dinners at
your house? Maybe restaurant management is something you should
consider. A good place to start might be local bars that host game nights,
or your favorite brunch places if evening hours are not appealing. Do
you like numbers and problem-solving as well as food? Maybe you want
to start looking into restaurant, retail, or grocery management, or even
jobs at large-scale production facilities, beginning with a junior-level
role in operations. Maybe you love to draw, or you're good with language, or you have a quick, cheeky wit. Every food business out there
needs a talented graphic designer, writer, or copy editor for their menus,
apps, signage, social media, packaging, and so much more, and there's
likely more than one business that shares your sense of aesthetics or
humor. The opportunities to be creative in the food world are off the

charts—and they aren't necessarily all culinary. So much imagination and personality go into the daily business of selling food. If this is your jam, there are many areas where you could learn the ropes and add tremendous value.

I noticed that I loved to cook and create new, unusual flavor combinations—an urge that could crop up suddenly and at strange times in the day. Rosemary and dark chocolate. *Dark chocolate and rosemary.* Wouldn't that spicy, woodsy, rosemary smell be sooo yummy if it were combined with dark, luxurious, rich, fruity chocolate? Out of the blue, I would be thinking about baking a cake like that. Sappy, syrupy, melty, gooey goodness. *Herbal chocolate infusion heaven.* It was moments like these that first made me think about the possibility of really becoming a chef.

What's on Your Wish List?

Getting to the bottom of what truly makes you happy demands that you pay close attention to those small, fleeting moments and the thoughts they bring, and then intentionally capturing those thoughts in your mind as they arise in the middle of your stressful, busy workday. Which they will, even at the crummiest of "crumby" jobs! If you can do that, you can target your next opportunities from a place of personal passion, and that in itself will place you far ahead of the curve.

Remember when I started working for that food broker as a teenager and learned all about the manufacturing and purchasing side of the industry? I realized that I loved connecting people through food and got a gnawing feeling I couldn't shake. That feeling eventually took me to Le Cordon Bleu, and later to that five-star hotel, and then to London, and then back to the US and Pasadena—and then to the decision to start all over yet again and dive into the jobs section on Craigslist? I mean, so, *so* many starts and restarts.

Everything that had happened in my career up to that point was driven by a combination of instinct, uncomfortable churning, and *ambition* in my belly; a willingness to try unknown and new things;

and gracious older mentors who inspired me to think about my future in ways I never had before. The sum of it all was incredibly valuable because I gained skills and experience and arrived at a point where I knew it was time to start taking control. So, I quit my exec chef job and decided to go all in on what was next. While I supported myself working as a private chef (along with that sometimes-porn-caterer work I mentioned), I made a list of all the things I wanted for my next role. It looked something like this:

Renee's Next-Job Wish List

- Get back to Europe

- Leadership with kindness and clear communication

- Opportunities for growth

- Food with specific values: organic and freshly prepared (non-negotiable!)

- Strategic and business thinking: tapping back into all the skills I learned early on, like negotiations, purchasing, contracts, business organization, and financials

- Reasonable quality of life, preferably no nights

- Paid time off for vacation

- Health benefits and a retirement fund

- Get back to Europe (did I say that already?)

What started to come into shape as I connected all these wishes was the idea of franchise operations. If I could find the right concept that matched my culinary values, it seemed like a good opportunity to learn the "business side" of food. It took a few months of searching, but eventually I found an ad for the position of a regional kitchen manager for the LA locations of a multi-unit restaurant concept.

"Most Definitely a Neurosis" Rosemary Dark Chocolate Cake

ALL IN TAKES ABOUT 50 TO 55 MINUTES *not including resting time*

ACTIVE TIME 30 MINUTES

MAKES 1 3-LAYER 9-INCH CAKE OR A BUNCH OF MINI CAKES

If you really like that rosemary flavor, you can boost it up further by infusing rosemary into some simple syrup and adding that to whipped cream as a topping. And here's another hot tip: if you reduce the amount of rosemary cream the recipe calls for and let it rest while you make the cake, you will finish the whole cake much faster.

Ganache

1½ cups heavy cream

4 branches rosemary, rinsed and dried

10 ounces semisweet chocolate chips *Callebaut again—for this one, use 54.5% dark.*

Cake

3 cups all-purpose flour

2 cups granulated sugar

1½ cups cocoa powder (100% cocoa—no sugar!)

1 tablespoon baking soda

1½ teaspoons baking powder

1½ teaspoons fine sea salt

4 large eggs, mixed well with fork

1½ cups buttermilk

1½ cups warm water

½ cup vegetable oil

2 teaspoons vanilla extract

If you have a large measuring cup, you can just measure the buttermilk, water, oil, and vanilla extract together and pour all into the mixing bowl at once when the recipe tells you to. Faster + Easier = Winning!

To prepare the ganache, warm the cream slowly with the rosemary in a small saucepan over low heat. Bring just to a boil, then reduce heat to low and reduce the cream by ¼. *Reducing the cream will make it more flavorful.*

Once the cream is reduced, let it sit, covered, for up to 2 hours for max flavor boost. Place chocolate in a medium heatproof bowl and hold aside until cake is baked.

Meanwhile, prepare your cake. Preheat oven to 350°F. Butter and flour 3 9-inch cake molds. *Sometimes I just use 2 to make really fat cakes because I like to use tiny ring molds to cut out tall mini layer cakes.*

Sift the dry ingredients (flour, sugar, cocoa, baking soda, baking powder, salt) directly into a stand mixer bowl and mix with paddle attachment until well combined. Add mixed eggs, buttermilk, warm water, oil, and vanilla in that order (or all at once if you have the big measuring cup!). Mix until combined and batter is smooth (approximately 2 minutes).

Divide batter among the prepared molds. Bake for 30 to 35 minutes or until a toothpick inserted into the center comes out clean. Remove from oven and cool on wire racks with a baking tray underneath. After a few minutes, remove cake from cake molds and let cool completely.

When ready to finish the ganache (because the cake is ready), reheat the cream just to a boil and immediately remove from the heat. Strain the cream over the chocolate to remove the rosemary. Cover the bowl tightly with aluminum foil and let it sit for 5 minutes. Stir with a heatproof spatula to melt the chocolate and fully incorporate the cream.

Voilà! Ganache!

With the cooled cakes still on the wire rack, pour warm ganache over the tops just to the edge and coat evenly. Let set, then stack! Decorate as you like. *I prefer mine plain and rustic, but you do you!*

I went through the hiring process and learned that the job checked off pretty much everything on my wish list. They offered me the role, which was exciting enough, but I was extra-proud of myself for negotiating a better salary and title—$55,000 plus bonus and California kitchen manager instead of LA kitchen manager. It was the start of a whole new phase in my career. Now I was managing multiple kitchens, not just one.

All the clues you need to direct your career are already inside you. You, and only you, know what you love about your job and what you don't. The only step that's left is to look for the places where your passion crosses with opportunity. A great way to begin, no matter where you are in your career, is to pin down your *dream* scenario so that you can start building toward it. Here are a few things to consider as you do that:

Time: How do you want to spend your free time? Do you like late nights, or do you or will you have kids at home that need to be taken care of in the evenings? Do you want to see the world and meet new people? Maybe you need flexible hours or a certain schedule to make your personal commitments work? Pay attention to that—it's one of the best gifts of the food world. Every possible shift you can imagine exists.

Benefits: Do you want health insurance that includes very specific things, like fertility coverage? Or perhaps you are really interested in tuition benefits. Go beyond the functional aspects of your potential career and starting thinking about your personal goals—what makes you happiest and feel the most energy when you think about the unique benefits that would enhance your life goals.

Happiness: Ask yourself what I call "joy questions," like:

- What do you want for your life?

- What do you feel most passionate about? What topics in the world are endlessly interesting to you? What subjects spark a fire in your belly?

- Why is the food industry interesting for you? What is it exactly that you love about food?

- Does it feed your soul to cook for and feed others? Or is it more about the art and experimentation? Or perhaps it's the financial wizardry behind the exciting challenge of making businesses with the smallest margins imaginable wildly profitable.

- How do you feel when someone else is satisfied and happy with a food experience you have created?

- Do you love people and find energy when you share stories and jokes and laugh together over snacks, drinks, and games?

- What makes you happiest, and where do you find joy in your own life?

Now, look at the jobs you've had so far and ask yourself some work-specific joy questions, calling up how you've felt as you've moved through your daily shifts:

- What do you love about the job?

- When do you feel happiest during the working day?

- What are things that you look forward to doing and are excited to help with when asked?

- What is your job missing? What do you wish you could do in your next job?

Keeping track of the things that bring you joy in the day-to-day, that make you feel happy and fulfilled, and then using the list to guide your next decision may not land you your dream job right now, but it will bring you closer and closer to that job with each step you take. You are basically reverse engineering your pathway to what will eventually become your dream job. And I can guarantee you that if you go through this process every year as a matter of personal career housekeeping, you will be stunned to see how your thinking evolves over the years as you learn more and gain new experiences.

No Joy? Listen to That, Too

Say, for example, you are a young man in high school in Hawaii and you get a job scooping ice cream at Baskin-Robbins. You like food, you like people, but you keep thinking about social justice issues. Plus, your wrists are starting to ache from all that ice cream scooping, so you leave the world of food, go to college, and end up becoming the president of the United States. Turns out, food was not Barack Obama's life's passion. But he still learned a lot from it by paying attention—he has spoken publicly about how that early food-industry job taught him a lot about responsibility and balancing work and friends, and how it gave him an opportunity to connect with his community.

And even though food *is* my life's passion, there have been plenty of times when I've felt far from passionate. When I was working as a line cook, I loved immersing myself in the fast, relentless rhythm of managing the garde-manger station (cold foods), working the fish station (despite the eyeball burning), or stepping in as backup on the grill—in those roles, hours could go by and I wouldn't even notice. On the other hand, I felt completely drained and uninspired when I "did my time" in the pastry department. Making batters and doughs all day, baking off enormous sheet-pan cakes and freezing them, and the precision and discipline you had to maintain in order to make *all* the different fillings, frostings, and cookies felt like watching cement dry. I could have sporked my own brain out. *Torture.*

Don't get me wrong. I did learn amazing recipes and techniques, like how to make the perfect crème brûlée and the importance of putting as much diplomat cream on everything you possibly can. Oh, and I became addicted to clotted cream. But otherwise, zero joy. I loved the energy and pace of cooking. *Fire and knives, baby!* Baking? Not so much. But, man, while I respect the hell out of anyone with those skills, I realized quickly that it wasn't for me, and you could even see that lack of connection and passion in my results. I wouldn't have known this about myself if I hadn't worked in the pastry department, because I crave just about everything sweet and scrumptious. Baked goods, ice cream, pastries, cookies, cake—just sign me up. But while I love to eat them, I seriously don't love making them all day.

Later, I was similarly shocked to feel so joyless so often when I took that role of executive chef in Pasadena. It had been my *dream job*. So why was I so damn miserable? I began to peel apart the things I loved and the things that exhausted me. I was working *all* the time and missed my friends and family. I was tired all the time. On the other hand, I loved the restaurant so much and the kitchen team was absolutely amazing. Every single person taught me something and worked incredibly hard to deliver meals with excellence and love. We laughed constantly and played pranks and just had fun.

I still think about that team all the time. (Mario, Nava, Luis, Juan, Sidronio, all of you: I love you dearly and hold you in my heart every single day.) These team members were some of the hardest-working, loveliest, most talented folks I have ever had the honor to work with over the course of my career. And yet, I was joyless in my work as it related to my personal life. I craved a middle ground, a work-life balance, and I would never have known this about myself if I hadn't discovered it as I experienced the job "in real time."

It's Easy to Quit—Much Harder to Stay (Yes, That Is Another Echo You Hear!)

Here's a tip: If you decide you need to quit immediately because you aren't feeling joy *around the clock*, then you are probably shooting yourself in the foot. You have to be "in it to win it," remember? You can't win the lottery if you never purchase the ticket—or, in this case, if you throw the ticket out before the numbers are called. It's the same with your career: you can't have the career of your dreams if you quit every job because you aren't hitting the joy jackpot right away. Staying power matters a lot in terms of building a career, so you need to tap into that discipline whenever possible as you figure out Plan B.

If you're not feeling happy at work, be strategic and use that time to educate yourself on what you do want, what you do like, and what exactly it is that you don't. Lean on your resilience muscle while you unpack those lessons, and start to get even more specific with your "joy questions." Ask yourself deeper things, like:

- Do I feel energized by the fast-paced, chaotic, "every moment is different" environment, or does it feel energy-sucking and deflating? Or is the environment dull, drab, and painfully slow? Am I yearning for more energy and connection?

- Am I enjoying being around people, working with and perhaps serving others? What are my favorite parts of that? What are my least favorite?

- What do I dread and truly despise the most about my current role and responsibilities?

- If my job feels too hard, what do I specifically mean by "hard"? Is it tedious? Challenging? Tiring? Is something chafing against my values or crossing my personal boundaries?

- Would improving my skills make the work feel easier, or is this something that can't be fixed through more training or experience?

- Do I hate the work or do I hate my colleagues? Dig deeply to understand "why." Or is the problem my boss? What would have to change for me to be happier in this role?

Even the most challenging and joyless work experiences you could possibly imagine can offer worthy lessons along the way. At one point in my early career, I had to deal with extreme and disgusting pest issues. I'm talking persistent and mind-blowing cockroach and mice invasions. I still vividly remember the customer who came in first thing one morning and ordered breakfast to go. He promptly returned ten minutes later to say that there was a cockroach "in there," pointing to his takeout bag. The manager called me over and I peeked inside the bag, where a cockroach was indeed hanging on the backside of this customer's breakfast for dear life, just like he was in the middle of free-climbing El Capitan. *So damn disgusting.*

The pest issue alone almost made me quit that job on the spot several times because the management team responsible didn't seem to have any sense of urgency around it *at all.* And, bizarrely, some of the customers didn't, either. On a different morning, just after the restaurant doors opened, a customer was picking up a breakfast item to take away, and a little mouse scurried right past him across the retail countertop. I think my eyes just about flew out of my head. I literally froze, just waiting for the inevitable disgust. I mean, in my opinion it would have been fully justified—I was horrified and seriously concerned about food safety and human health, not to mention damage to the business's reputation. But the customer only looked at the barista, shrugged his shoulders, turned on his heels *with* his purchase, and walked out. *Huh?*

I did everything you can possibly imagine trying to mitigate these issues, but we humans were totally outnumbered by the critters. It was like trying to fight a war with a toothpick. Once I felt I had exhausted all of the possible pathways for a sustainable solution, I ended up compiling the numerous email chains to management and an outline of every single instance and discussion related to the topic and passed it on to the most senior leader I knew. It was basically a last-ditch Hail Mary to get some action. All it did was get me in some serious hot water about how I, personally, was "not handling the issue properly." Why couldn't I get anyone to take care of it? What was wrong… *with me*? That was a curveball I didn't see coming and, frankly, it absolutely crushed me. That was my last hope.

So why did I care so much if no one else really did? Because I was the one who had to stand there in the middle of a fully packed restaurant with a broomstick in hand trying to ensure a rat the size of my foot wasn't going to come back out from under the counter until after the lunch rush was over. *Yep—guardian of the rodents, that was me.* I mean, this wasn't real life *Ratatouille*—this was absolutely shameful. That's when I made the private decision to leave this particular business—I felt like my own professional reputation was going to be damaged by the inaction of others and at the expense of trusting customers. *But I still had bills to pay! Gah!*

It took many months to find the right next job—and in the meantime, I hung in there and stayed with it. (*Thanks again, resilience muscle!*) I even got promoted in the midst of it all. Which is exactly the point I am trying to make. I stayed until I had the *right* next move, and in staying, good career things happened.

You Can't Separate Your Joy from Your Values

While you are paying attention to what you love about your job and what you can't stand, don't forget to also pay attention to *who you are*. Your values and what you hold dear will always be your critical North Star in your personal career journey, guiding your decision-making toward roles that are more and more aligned with what you want for yourself. And make no mistake about it: Your values are going to evolve and mature throughout your career journey. That's normal and expected! What I care about now is vastly different from what I cared about when I first started out. I grew so much through experience and especially through my learning moments, and that evolution is what's important in shaping and defining what is important to you. As you go through this journey—especially in your early career days—you are going to encounter all sorts of moments when your "values line" gets crossed. But these are the moments that will help you gain clarity on what your true values are and why they matter to you. These moments and the lessons you take from them will make you a stronger professional and better colleague, and they will inform the behaviors of future-leader you. The power of these line-crossing moments is real.

That pest experience, for example, stayed with me in all of my later roles and leadership decisions and led me to heavily invest in food and workplace safety programs in the operations I oversaw to ensure it never got that bad. Over the next many years, I shared that story with team members who had to solve similar issues—unfortunately, dealing with pests is a reality of the food world—to help them see that these issues are entirely solvable with the right partners, tactical strategy, and investments at the table. Even as a business owner today, I still support clients with food and workplace safety strategies and execution: it is a critical and continuous theme, and always a high priority for serious business leaders. Truth be told, I don't know that I would feel nearly as passionate about it if I hadn't done my time as "guardian of the rodents."

But that's the magic at work, isn't it? It's why the hard stuff matters more than the easy stuff. I absolutely love talking about pest mitigation strategies now, as well as working on projects that transform behaviors and spaces for the better. It actually brings me a sense of joy and deep personal satisfaction to know I am contributing to a safer, cleaner, pest-free food experience.

So, now that we are crystal clear on how your joy and values are interconnected, how does that combination inform optimal career decision-making as you consider what's important to you? Let me tell you about one of the key takeaways I earned from my time as a culinary student in France. I came to understand that, as a chef, I wanted to make dishes that are prepared thoughtfully and delicately with ingredients that are fresh, transparent, and obvious. And while I adored the food in Europe, I also realized along the way that I needed to apply those French techniques in a much lighter style, because eating rich food all day (every day!) was not making me *feel* good. So, I made it my personal cooking mantra that I would only make food I would serve to my own grandmother. That was the bar. Would I be proud to serve it to Emilie? And, further, would Emilie approve?

That inner promise went way beyond ingredients—Emilie was a woman who sprinkled dried parsley on every plate because she thought things should always look beautiful, and who kept a radio tuned to the public classical music station in every room of the house because it was "just nice to walk into a room and hear beauty." The unique and exceptionally high standards she modeled for me translated into culinary principles like creating stunning, breathtaking food experiences and plate presentations, uncompromising ingredient quality standards, and deliberate portion sizes, as well as building every recipe with a sense of curiosity, imagination, and wonder. I wanted my culinary influence to not only be memorable but also make others *feel* good in every way. I wanted to ignite and delight all the senses, not just one or two. So, I kept Emilie as my invisible sit-on-the-shoulder Supreme Court Justice through every quality and value decision I made in my career, and I keep her there to this day. Let me put it this way: armed with these particular culinary and experience values, I sought work only with organizations who seemed aligned with those same values. Delivering fresh, delicious, and nutritionally balanced food in awesome environments and in all sorts of ways brought me great and satisfying joy. That mattered to me—and whatever it is that matters to you will help you navigate your career choices in ways you can't yet imagine.

So, as you determine for yourself how you are going to show up as an employee, a coworker, and, eventually, a leader, who is it in your life that can act as your own invisible guide? What values will you discover inside yourself as you notice and examine the moments in your workdays that make you feel tired, tense, or uncomfortable, and the ones that make you feel energized, joyful, and connected, as if you are an important part of something great and meaningful? All of those feelings are your actual career road map, so follow them wisely. Commit to that and you'll end up exactly where you are meant to be—joy, values, and all.

TIME TO GET INTO MISE MODE

**Your prep for navigating by joy all the way
to your true food-world happy place.**

MINDSET SHIFT: Don't let the highs and lows you experience over your working day just *happen* to you—use them as your teacher and guide. When are you in the flow? When are you dragging your feet? This information can help you determine your next steps.

TRADE SECRET: Make a list of what you need in your life—at home and in your career. Some employers have a ton of resources, perks, and benefits available *for free* to help support you and meet the needs that matter most to you: paid tuition, health and fertility benefits, parental leave programs—you name it. So, take a hard, close look at what's available when you're deciding what moves to make (if any).

LEADERSHIP LOWDOWN: It's not just the entry-level jobs that can leave you feeling, well, less than joyful. Be prepared to hit that wall throughout your career—just remember to leave strategically and to learn everything you can before you do. "It's easy to leave, much harder to stay"—but staying is where you will learn the most as you line up what's next. So be disciplined and put yourself and your career goals first.

INSIDER DISH

*More expert info?
Amazing! This way!*

Part Two

TAKING YOUR PLACE AT THE MANAGERS' TABLE

BEYOND THE PREP STATION
Moving up into Management

If you are intentional about how you want to be known, you will be far more likely to achieve the impact and leadership legacy you want.

THE CAREER MOMENT you have been waiting for and working toward has finally arrived. All of your incredibly hard work is finally paying off. *This right here.* This is where you enter the next phase of your career journey. Congratulations on earning a seat at the management table!

When you reach this point, it's really important to take a pause and just allow yourself to feel proud of everything you've done so far in your career and everything you've walked through to get here. *You stayed in it*—and now you are a warrior, headed toward a place where you can have a positive impact not only on the team you oversee, but also on the *entire industry*, and in so many ways. Take the win, celebrate, and really enjoy this milestone. You deserve it and you have a lot of work to do, so it's important to mark this moment in your life in a sweet and memorable way.

While this might seem like an odd way to start our conversation about moving up to management, it's actually a key part of your new role and future work. *Acknowledgment.* Taking the time to mark success for yourself and others. We all get so caught up in the warp speed of the day-to-day that it's easy to lose sight of why we are all here and what it's all for. What does success even mean to you? And can you really appreciate your hard-earned accomplishments if you're not stopping to honor them? And here's a bigger question: If you aren't able to do this for yourself, how can you purposefully do it for others? See where I am going with this?

Practice the Art of Celebrating Wins

The ability to acknowledge and celebrate wins, and especially the achievements of others who have mightily contributed to *your* wins, is what sets apart the truly great leaders from the "meh" ones. You are fully in the people business now. Thinking about the experience of others is one of the most impactful things you can do as you move into higher levels of management and, eventually, leadership. And as we know from watching any Super Bowl, all the best coaches know how to celebrate.

So how will you do it? Some people buy cool toys to mark landmark career moments. Make no mistake: any new job, promotion, certification, a "no accidents in a month" day—you name it, it is a landmark moment. Even a daily performance marker like getting through an endless holiday meal service, or packaging up that thousandth meal, or wrapping up a tough financial period on target (weekly, monthly, quarterly, or annually) is worthy of acknowledgment and recognition.

You could even buy yourself an enormous TV, upgrade to the newest iPhone, or take a long weekend. I've seen colleagues do all these things to mark a personal win. In terms of your team, a lot of great managers I've worked with and for have made it a point to acknowledge the successes of their employees with small, meaningful gestures like a handwritten card or a token gift. And because we are food people, the most common celebration is going to involve, well, food. *Because it's just so delicious when you get there.* For me, it's all about the wine. I just love the anticipation of selecting a special or unusual bottle to share with loved ones, as well as the moment when we can all sit down together, relax, and laugh over a meal until the wee hours of a morning.

You'll find your own way to mark your moment when it comes. After all, it all starts with yourself. *So, go forth and celebrate in whatever way works for you.* Champion. Acknowledge. Savor.

Are You Ready to Walk Your "I'd Do Things Differently" Talk?

All right, all right, let's wrap up the celebrating for a moment. You're a manager now, after all, and you have a team to support! In my work as a leader, whenever I'm coaching a team member who has an eye on management, I usually like to start with one question: "What do you think management is?" The answers are always eye-opening—it's not unusual to hear back that management is "telling people what to do and that they have to do it" or something along that line. The thing is, I used to feel pretty much the same way a thousand years ago, which is why that answer always cracks me up. It all looked so easy... what could possibly be difficult? You just tell people what to do and they do it. It's not like it's brain surgery. Well, actually... it's not that far off—*actual scalpel sometimes required!*

Management is not "telling people what to do." It's the art of working with people in order to collectively act and behave in alignment toward accomplishing the goals of the business. In other words, it's finding ways to work with people and joining forces to get the job done. It's not about knowing each and every piece of the puzzle; it's about collaborating with others to solve issues and accomplish the defined objectives of the organization. It's important to understand this so that we can talk about how you should approach your new role and what you need to keep in mind. It's especially all about relationships and targets. It's about how you understand your role and responsibilities and, in turn, how you motivate and inspire others to meet those obligations. All of this can sound a little intimidating, so think of it this way: you are now a paid problem-solver and you have a set of goals you need to meet that you can accomplish only by working with others. That's it.

Once you're in charge of making things happen in your part of the food world, you're going to feel pressure in a whole different way. Whether you're a new supervisor, team leader, or manager, you are now directly responsible for a large part of the experience that others are having in their day-to-day work environment. Oh, and you're also accountable for the performance of your team—you know... the actual *results* part. As they say, "Shit's about to get real."

It's time to ask yourself what kind of boss you will be: Will you be the one who screams and belittles your team to get the aisle cleaned, boxes moved, or bread sliced? Or the one who listens to your employees, hears their challenges, and finds ways to improve the work experience for everybody's mutual benefit, all while keeping the business goals you've been charged with on track? Successful management takes some "next level" multitasking, so this is the moment when you will take your collective learnings from every role you've had up to this point and start being intentional about how you are going to be known as a leader.

Remember all those super-challenging bosses and colleagues I faced while I was cooking in Europe? I learned incredible things there, but it came at such a price. It took so much energy every day just to tolerate that kind of environment. I felt nameless and faceless in so many of those roles—it was humiliating and demoralizing to realize that I was just another pair of hands to my management, and they were not interested in what I had to say. Imagine what the results could have been if I had been able to harness that energy and direct it toward the success of the organization instead of spending it on muttering "I will not quit" to myself a thousand times a day. Instead of bringing new ideas to the table—like the most badass chilled soup you've never had before (all made from scraps of sole bones and smoked salmon trimmings designated for the trash bin)—I kept my head down and mouth shut. *Chef did not want to hear about my creations, no matter how awesome or profitable they might turn out to be.* That soup was unique and could have been an amazing signature dish to bring to customers—and it would have been a cash cow because it was almost entirely made from food waste. But instead, it stayed in my personal recipe vault. What a business opportunity miss.

At that time in my life, I was sparking with creative energy like an obsessed, mad culinary scientist, but I had no safe pathway to bring any of those ideas forward. The environment created by my leaders was intense, cutthroat, and fueled with high-octane intimidation in the relentless pursuit of culinary excellence, and the result was stifling, not motivating. Creativity, excitement, and innovation were sidelined in favor of a "don't think, just do what you're told" approach. As a manager, you can be different. If you understand and embrace the fact that you are in a position to not just recognize that spark in your team but also actually nurture it into a flame, the creative energy in your team will become *your* creative energy, too, and those successes and first-ever innovations will become feathers in *your* management cap. And your customers will get some awesome experiences! Win, win, *win*! Those are the lessons I took with me into management.

That period permanently marked me and informed so much of the leader I became. My experiences made me think about what I would do differently when I was the boss and inspired me to begin reading leadership books and seek out successful professionals who were willing to share personal experiences from when they were climbing the ranks. Those mentors told me about the hard times they had encountered, the best and the worst jobs and bosses they ever had (and why), and how those experiences impacted them. They all had one thing in common: candidly, they focused on their own leadership development and continued learning. It made them better leaders, and ultimately it made their team performance stronger, which showed in the business results. Frankly, it was these conversations that gave me the strength to stay in some of my most difficult jobs and take the learnings. Sometimes, just knowing that people you respect have been through what you've been through can be the fuel you need to keep trudging through. Especially when things get weird—which they absolutely will in management.

Yes, Shit Is About to Get Weird— So Get Your PBOD Together Now

"Morning team! So, just a small update for you as you start your shift today. Jason, our talented IT guru, shagged a customer on the barista counter last night and it was captured on the security camera, so we had to fire him. What a moron—hope the sexy time was worth it! Anyway, have a great day! Go team!"

Ever heard something like that in a meeting? *OMG, I seriously hope not.* Your organization is relying on managers like you (yes—that is, or will be, literally *you*) to set an example, make good judgment calls, be professionally mature, and steer everything in the direction of success. So you can't exactly call your team into a meeting and say something like this. I mean, I suppose you could, but it would probably be your last meeting at the company and you would be joining "randy Jason" in the unemployment line. You would also be distracting the business by creating a firestorm of gossip and chatter. Which, of course, translates to lower team productivity.

Instead, you might hear, or say, something like this: "I have some unfortunate news to share. Jason, our IT guru, has decided to leave his position, effective immediately, for personal reasons. Please reach out to his teammate, Susan, while we work through this transition, to support your tech needs. We will miss Jason and his valuable contributions to the business very much and wish him so well in his new endeavors. I know that's a lot of news for today, but we need to stay on track. It's going to be a busy morning, so let's get going and refocus our energy on the tasks at hand."

Over the course of your career in the food world, you will find yourself in many unbelievably tricky, inappropriate, and downright strange situations. It's the "people business" after all, remember? There will be some wild employee circumstances that come across your desk that you may never have seen or experienced before. I mean, the stuff movies are made of. Remember, there is always a first time for everything. Things like no-shows, when team members decide without telling anyone not to come in for their shift one day—or ever again. Surprisingly, this—a "full ghosting," if you will—isn't uncommon. Maybe a staff member decides to leave or quit mid-shift. Sometimes arguments that have nothing to do with work are brought into the workplace (like folks fighting over fantasy football gone wrong), and you have to get involved to prevent it from impacting performance. An employee might fake a disability and get busted at the grocery store by his colleagues; another might be drunk or on drugs (or both) on the job. You will probably have to deal with people stealing food, money, or drinks.

And it's not just the floor-level staff who bring the drama. Sometimes it's your boss, or your boss's boss. I know of a senior executive at a major global food chain who lost his job for "bumping naughties" on company premises after hours. Ridiculous stuff happens more than you think. Maybe a restaurant manager is falsely posing as a doctor in his leisure time and gets caught when an employee runs into him at a nightclub. Or a manager orders a bunch of produce and meat and has it delivered to his secret side business.

Sometimes it's plain old bad personal hygiene that finds its way into your orbit—like the overwhelming stench of farts in meetings (*and yes, we all know who is doing it!*) or body odor that's so strong, people in the room have to excuse themselves. Unfortunately, as a manager, you will likely end up having to hold one of the most awkward conversations of your life discussing personal hygiene and deodorant with the stinky culprit after the inevitable employee and customer complaints.

You will even encounter moments that are potentially life-threatening, like when one employee thought it would be smart to bring a BB gun to work and start shooting pigeons off the roof of a loading dock, all while America's schools were going through active shooter drills every other day and everyone on the team was already terrified of workplace violence. *But nope, let's bring a big rifle-looking gun to work and blast pigeons! In the name of food safety! That won't scare anyone!* No matter what happens, you have to deal with it all professionally, especially as you climb the ranks of leadership.

In any of these scenarios, your most critical source of support (outside of a really strong, capable DEI & Talent team) will be a network of safe and reliable mentors who can be called upon for advice and wise counsel. These are people who have walked in your shoes before and gained the experience and perspective to help you navigate all of these uncharted waters. It's impossible to count the times in my career when I had to call someone and say, "I can't believe this happened. I don't even know what to do." I mean, sometimes I was making "WTF is this bullshit" calls to my mentors daily.

If you can gather together such a team, you will have someone on hand who can tell you the truth, guide you toward a greater understanding of the challenges your people are facing in their roles, and advise you on how to deal with them with fairness, compassion, and professionalism. Perhaps most importantly, they can give you a safe, confidential outlet to just get it all out. Everyone needs to share with someone. And the higher up you go, the lonelier it gets because you have to really think about whom you can safely share private company business with. *Not many.* This is a reality that many people don't consider as they head into management.

Start forming your safety net of sympathetic, experienced, and knowledgeable counselors during the early stage of your management journey. They will become your own "Personal Board of Directors" over time. Every successful leader of any business has a PBOD behind them, and the more skilled, experienced, and supportive they are, the more they will have a positive impact on your career. Oh, and just know that the challenges will only get more astonishing and intense as your career moves forward, so identifying wise folks and fostering long-term relationships with them now, in the beginning, is actually professional development mastery in action. Your end reward? A reliable team of career champions who will listen well, provide insightful professional solutions, hold your feet to the fire when it's necessary (because no one is perfect!), and call you to your best self.

In fact, a lot of people pay for personal career or executive coaching just to gain access to this type of safe, confidential, experienced counsel on a regular basis. (I even offer this myself through my consulting firm.) You can skip those kinds of bills by intentionally and proactively identifying mentors *now*, at the beginning of your management journey, and continually investing in your PBOD so that you have access to this kind of leadership at your fingertips whenever you need it going forward.

When all is said and done, I feel that I owe my career success to my PBOD, and I carry them in my heart with gratitude every day. You would not even believe some of the things they have had to listen to and counsel me through over the years, but let's just say that there is literally a first time for everything. *And I mean, everything. You'll see.*

So, What Does It Actually Mean to Be a Good Manager?

As you find your footing in this new role, you'll be wise to create a core list of attributes that are important to you, and that's true whether you're launching into management in a brand-new company or you've moved up the ladder under the same employer. If you want to actually receive the respect you need to get the job done, you need to be *worthy* of that respect in all aspects of your behavior. Respect is difficult to gain, as we all know, and it is extremely easy to lose. But even by thinking about the leadership qualities you most admire—and the ones you most detest—you will start to inform and shape your own leadership style. Right from the beginning, it's important to be intentional about how you are going to show up for your team as a manager. Small, simple gestures will help you build that respect over the long term.

So how do you start? You start by thinking about the people who have inspired you over the years and all of the qualities you admire most in them. There are your old bosses, of course, but leaders can come in many forms—teachers, athletic coaches, aunts and uncles, colleagues, even your best friend's grandma or maybe that lady who is always holding court in the neighborhood coffee shop. Think about who among all the people in your life has qualities you respect and write those attributes down. Then, think further out: Who have you seen on TV or TikTok or read about that exemplifies the values you respect? Is it José Andrés, Martha Stewart, or Marcus Samuelsson? Maybe it's Elon Musk or Alexandria Ocasio-Cortez. What are the leadership qualities among your favorite heroes or achievers (those who motivate you, those you respect for whatever reason) that speak to you personally? Write them down, too.

Now, flip the pancake. Think of the qualities in leaders you have despised. Why didn't their style work for you? Write about that.

"Absolutely Delightful" Grilled Chicken Cobb Salad with Perfectly Boiled Eggs *FFS!*

ALL IN TAKES ABOUT 50 TO 55 MINUTES • ACTIVE TIME 15 MINUTES

MAKES 4 STUNNING SALADS OR 1 GINORMOUS PLATTER

If you believe the folklore, the Cobb salad originated in the 1930s in Hollywood at the Brown Derby restaurant, when Mr. Cobb threw together a bunch of cold leftovers from the fridge late one evening. Whatever the true origin, hands down, it's my favorite salad. That it was potentially made while scrounging around a fridge late one evening just cracks me up and makes me love it even more. I mean, who hasn't done that once or twice?

Salad

16 ounces baby gem hearts or romaine lettuce, washed, dried, and chopped into small ribbons (no stems!)

Maldon salt and freshly ground black pepper, to your taste

3 to 4 chicken breasts, freshly grilled with salt and pepper and chopped into small cubes
Yes, you want these warm if possible... it's just better.

6 strips bacon, cooked and diced small

4 large tomatoes, diced into small cubes (you could sub cherry tomato halves)

6 hard-boiled eggs, quartered or sliced into strips on an old-school egg slicer

2 ripe avocados, peeled and diced
Do this only when ready to assemble salads, so the avocado doesn't discolor.

1 cup blue cheese, hand crumbled
Fourme d'Ambert is my fave, although Roquefort and Stilton are hard to beat.

126

Balsamic Vinaigrette

½ cup high-quality balsamic vinegar

1 tablespoon Dijon mustard

¾ cup high-quality extra-virgin olive oil

Maldon salt and freshly ground black pepper

To make the dressing, whisk together the vinegar and mustard in a small bowl. Add the olive oil slowly while whisking to thicken the dressing. Finish with Maldon and black pepper, to taste. You can store this in the fridge for up to 3 days.

To make the salad, first make sure all of your ingredients are ready to go. Place greens in the bottom of a bowl. Season the lettuce with Maldon and pepper and toss to distribute evenly. *Yes, really... always season your greens!*

Evenly portion and create colorful rows of ingredients across the top of each salad (whether you are making individual portions or one big dish) in the following order: chicken, bacon, tomato, eggs, avocado, blue cheese. The most important thing is that you fully cover the lettuce, and you have different colors next to each other so that the salad looks visually stunning.

Serve with Maldon and a pepper grinder on the table along with the vinaigrette. Enjoy!

Here's a simple example of how this list worked for me. I had so many chefs who would come into the kitchen, bark orders, and then disappear until service time. I hated that experience and wanted to make sure my team knew I was there and available. That ended up becoming one of my core leadership principles throughout my career—*show up and show that you care*—and it was something I strived for from the time of my first management role. When you experience leaders who are not willing to do the tough jobs, or even just show up in small ways, you can feel the subsequent lack of respect and hard feelings that follow, and it makes things hard for everyone. I never wanted people to doubt my commitment to our shared success.

When I was working as an executive chef, one of the ways I tried to earn respect from my team was by being one of the first to arrive at work in the morning so that I could greet everyone as they entered the kitchen and bring that energy to the environment. At night, I would also stay in the kitchen until dinner service was finished so that I could offer the team a cold brew after the last plate went out and congratulate them on another successful service. I wanted everyone to know that I would never ask them to do anything I wasn't willing to do myself, so I pulled the same long hours they did. I knew that I was able to be successful in my role only because of the amazing team who was lifting me up.

There were a few unintended benefits to this along the way that I didn't anticipate. I was able to have direct, personal relationships with each person on my team, to see their challenges with fresh eyes and help remove roadblocks to make their jobs easier and more efficient. Plus, just by being there, I could catch recipe execution errors before they affected our service. On one particularly busy brunch, for example, I helped avert a crisis over hard-boiled eggs gone wrong: an entry-level cook had completely wrecked the eggs for the gorgeous grilled chicken Cobb salad. He thought his task was done, but the eggs were *way* overcooked and the yolks were a hideous, almost furry-looking greenish-black. *So gross.* I was able to make it a teaching moment, have the coaching conversation so this cook never made that mistake again, and correct the issue, saving the team from a service-time disaster. I think the Cobb salad was $20 at the time—can you imagine paying that much money for a salad with hideous eggs? Or waiting fifteen excruciatingly long minutes while new eggs were boiled, cooled, peeled, and brought to you? *Hard no.*

If you are intentional about how you want to be known, you will be far more likely to achieve the impact and leadership legacy you want. Really think about it and then drive your actions through this lens so that you are behaving in the way you intend from the start. Your list of desired attributes will remind you to bring your best to your work, especially in the hardest, darkest moments. You will find that if you reference this list for even a moment (as I have done in many bathroom stalls across the globe) before any tough conversation or decision-making crossroad, it will help you see through the trees and call you to your best self. You won't always get it right or act perfectly, but you will, at the very least, be proud of your own behavior and its impact on those around you.

Know What Your Job Is . . . Seriously!

There's a final "first step" for moving into management, and while it sounds obvious, it's actually more complicated than you'd think: *know the role and responsibilities of your new job.* It might surprise you that I have to say this, but you'll soon find out that the scope of your role and what you are tasked with accomplishing is not always clear—especially when you're first getting started. If you work in a restaurant and have been promoted to a shift manager or supervisor, for example, your new responsibilities might include things like opening the restaurant early in the morning to let your staff in and get the place ready for service, but you may also be tasked with finding ways to save on labor or other costs, and you might not have anticipated that demand. (I vividly remember watching a cook throw away an entire tray of burned sausages and then start over without a thought about the costs involved. All he needed was a timer, but he didn't have one and didn't know to ask for one. Simple things like that add up to big money over time!) Or remember that refrigerated packing room I mentioned earlier? If you are a new line manager at a production facility, you could be responsible for an area like that. You will certainly have productivity targets to make sure your team packages a certain number of dishes by a particular time, but it will also be your job to make sure everyone is following proper food handling practices, wearing safety and thermal gear, and that they are all compliant with time card and scheduled breaks policies, and other administrative responsibilities.

Maybe you're the new manager of a bakery? Then you might be tasked with reducing overtime costs and minimizing food waste while keeping the facility spotless, the operations seamless, and the display case full. In any of these positions, you're also likely to be tasked with multiple points of quality control, so you will need to know what those specific responsibilities are and how to execute them. And then there is always the drive for increasing revenue and achieving new sales targets. "Would you like some lemon almond cake with that cup of coffee, sir?" It's not just a thoughtful (and delicious) question; it serves a real business purpose, and gentle suggestions like this can help you steer your team toward achieving your collective goals.

Once you have prepared yourself to look for opportunities to accomplish what you've been tasked with doing, you will see them everywhere. But first, you need to understand your role and all of the responsibilities it entails to ensure that your focus stays on the right business priorities. Do that and it will keep your business moving forward. And guess what? It will keep *your* career moving forward, too.

TIME TO GET INTO MISE MODE

**Your prep for setting off on the right foot
as you enter into management.**

MINDSET SHIFT: True leadership isn't about telling people what to do. It's a collaborative *conversation* you are constantly holding with your team. That dynamic will allow you to work together to hit your performance goals while creating space for growth and innovation.

TRADE SECRET: Whatever you're going through, know that managers up the ladder have gone through it, too. Seek out mentors and get your "Personal Board of Directors" together, whether that's leaders in your own company or somewhere else. Your PBOD will give you the perspective you need to shine through the tough moments.

LEADERSHIP LOWDOWN: Knowing your role and responsibilities will keep you personally on track and delivering the results you need to keep moving forward in your career. Be clear about what you will need to deliver and what success looks like as you're doing it—for you, your business, and your team.

INSIDER DISH

Seriously impactful
"insights alert"!

8

THE MANAGEMENT BIG FIVE

Balancing the Flavor of Leadership

Nothing is simply what it is—there are sides, reasons, and perspectives to everything.

THE MOST INCREDIBLE, memorable chefs in the world are able to balance their plates masterfully between the five basic tastes: sweet, salty, bitter, sour, and umami. *The Big Five.* Chefs who get this wrong don't last very long. The way a dish is balanced is "make or break" in terms of whether a patron will enjoy the experience and whether they will love it enough to come back in search of more.

There's a second Big Five that every food business in every sector of the industry has to balance successfully as well: sight, sound, smell, taste, touch—the five basic human senses. Whether it's packaged cookies from Mondelēz, or gorgeous, fresh bowls from Chopt Creative Salad Company, or a plate of butter-poached lobster from your favorite fine dining restaurant, they all have to deliver these five experiences brilliantly if the business is going to survive over the long term. *Everything communicates* in the world of food, so things like packaging, design, materials, lighting, furniture, the sound of a bite or of a room, and so many others factors all matter just as much as how a given dish looks and tastes. You and I could have an endless conversation about the various sensory touch points that affect the customer experience and the very real business purpose behind most of it. (Like the fact that hard, uncomfortable seating is sometimes intentional. Yep. True!) But for the purpose of this exercise, let's boil it down to this: *Balancing the sensory, human experience matters enormously in the food world, and the intentionality behind it is fierce.*

And that brings us to yet *another* Big Five, and this one is all about you, your career, and how well you can align your efforts to meet these critical demands:

1 The needs of the business
2 The needs of your bosses
3 The needs of your customers
4 The needs of your team
5 And, finally, the needs of yourself

I call these the Management Big Five. These business pillars make up the lens you need to look through every time you make a decision in management. When you step into the role of manager, you'll soon learn that keeping them in balance is the difference between amateur hour and respected professionalism.

I remember being struck by how heavy, and sometimes impossible, it felt as I realized I had to consider all of these different and complex areas and relationships on top of the other Big Fives in my professional life. I mean, was I supposed to become a professional juggler all of the sudden? *How many balls of thoughtful consideration can one actually keep in the air?* As it turns out, quite a few.

The understanding that the game had changed—along with the criteria for success by which my performance was going to be measured—was a defining moment in my career. So please allow me to share this hard-earned pearl of wisdom with you. Once you step out of hourly roles and into a salaried role, the way your performance is going to be judged will make a complete pivot. It is no longer about what you can do with your own bare hands. *Welcome to management.*

Timing Is Everything

So how can you prepare to balance the Management Big Five in practical, everyday terms? It starts from the moment you begin your new role. Scratch that: it starts from your first interview. So pay attention to those vibes, and pay attention to the vibes you experience during your onboarding, too.

Yes, onboarding! Let's take a moment to talk about that. I love the word "onboarding." It sounds so fancy and exciting, and it's equal parts mystery and obvious: *the process of starting a new role*. Depending on the company you work for, it can be as simple as a small tour of the business, collecting a badge, and being told to just "jump in," or, with more developed organizations, it can be a multiday process full of presentations and training, company handbook sign-outs, tax and benefit documents, one-to-one meetings with key colleagues, and all sorts of other planned activities—even getting some swag—to get you immersed in the company culture and inspired for action as you dip your toe into the culture of your new employer.

The onboarding period is the time to settle in, learn the ropes, create relationships, and make sure that you understand your goals and deliverables. It's also your first real opportunity to gather your intel on how the Management Big Five are at play in this new environment, and what kind of an impact you might have on that balance. One of the most impactful things you can do when you start any new management role—and this goes even for executive-level work—is write down all the things you notice in your first week or two that should be different, or that you would like to correct or upgrade. Basically, make a list of the items you think could be more successful if only X happened. I call this the Pocket List. You will forget very quickly what you would change or do differently as you become familiar with your new environment and it all becomes the "new normal." The first week or two on the job is the only time when everything new will stand out to you in such a clear and obvious way—so capture it all.

Now, you are going to have opinions about *everything*. Of course, you will . . . you are human! But now is not the time to change things or throw the existing management balance out of whack. The most typical pitfall of early management jobs is changing things before you have the support of your boss or team. Activating your inner detective "on the regular" is key because, as you will discover, there are layers to everything. Nothing is simply what it is—there are sides, reasons, and perspectives to everything, and it's up to you to gather all of those puzzle pieces and put together a view of what's really happening in the business. Then, and only then, can you effectively determine and start to execute what *needs* to happen.

Don't believe me? Maybe you're thinking, "Aw, Renee, you're just talking about *other* people. I'm different. I'm smarter. I know best how things should be done." Well, take a moment to consider this scenario:

Rookie Manager (Inside Voice): Hmmm . . . the sales counter with the register seems so cluttered and all of the "impulse purchase" snacks are piled on top of each other. How can the customers even know what there is to get excited about? This needs to change at once.

Rookie Manager (Outside Voice): Hey team, can you move off all of the countertop items right away and find a flat basket or container so that you can more clearly lay out the snack options?

Rookie manager turns on heels and leaves in search of the next issue like a problem-solving machine.

Response from Team (Outside Voice): Sure.

Response from Team (Inside Voice): What a moron. If she had only asked why we do this, she would know that it's a personal pet peeve of the CEO to not have piles and hills of everything on the counter, so we are asked to do it like this. Now the new lady is asking for the opposite. What should we do? I don't want to get in trouble! I will just say okay and see what happens—I don't want to tell her!

See what happened here?

You—that rookie manager—had a good observation, and a thoughtful reason for wanting to change things directly (increasing sales). But you *never asked why* the current situation was the way it was in the first place. So now you have to get schooled by either your employees or your CEO when she finds out that you changed her preferred setup. From the perspective of the Management Big Five, you're already challenged. There's no sales shift yet in either direction, but your boss is going to be irritated, your customers will notice a change that may or may not affect their behavior, your team has doubts about your leadership, and you're in the eye of the storm and don't even know it. *Whoops.*

Timing really is everything. You don't need to address and fix each thing you notice as soon as you notice it. And if you aren't curious— if you don't ask questions and don't consider all of the underlying reasons before taking action—you will undermine your credibility and set yourself back. So. See something? Write it down on your Pocket List and keep moving forward. Yes, your list will grow and grow... and that is a very good thing.

When you get further into your role, or even to the next levels of management, that's when you can reference your list and do something about it. At that point, you will understand the landscape well enough that you can make improvements your colleagues will be grateful for, rather than resent. Plus, your bosses will notice that you were paying attention and looking for inefficiencies even while you were learning the ropes. Oh, and by sleuthing well, you will also get off on the right foot with your team because they will appreciate your questions and inquiries and feel like welcome partners in the journey. That's how new teams gel and trust gets established, which is a foundation you will need for all the work ahead.

Brewmaster, Mixologist, Bartender, Server

When thinking about the Management Big Five, it can help to imagine the most badass selection of custom beer tap handles you have ever seen. You know that moment when you walk into a bar and see a row of really cool handles that are just begging to be pulled? As you get to know a business and all of its priorities, values, and goals—including those of your boss, team, and customers—imagine yourself as the bartender, pushing and pulling these taps like levers in the effort to strike the right balance: *performance, relationships, performance, relationships, performance, relationships*. It's not a one-size-fits all situation, just like there isn't only one beer option in the world. There are thousands of beers with completely different recipes and flavor profiles because there are thousands of different preferences. As a manager, it's your job to figure out how to serve up the perfect "brew" that will meet the goals of the business and satisfy the tastes of every human involved. Understanding this critical dynamic will set you apart from your peers.

Back when I lived in London, there was a fairly common recipe that could be found on most daily menus that always left me feeling pretty *meh* about the whole thing. *Cold turkey curry, baby.* I found it consistently flat, dull, and one-dimensional and always in desperate need of whatever chutney was being served alongside to give it a little personality. Basically edible... *but why?* That is, until one day when I tasted a turkey curry sandwich in one of our locations and the creaminess of the mayo that coated the turkey chunks rolled perfectly over my tongue, and the spicy Madras curry blend alongside the fresh and unexpected zing of a truly bright, dynamic hint of citrus jolted my senses awake. Lemony, creamy, spicy, hearty? Who knew turkey curry could be so supremely awesome? It was a very pleasant surprise.

This recipe became a regular menu item at the business I was working for, and it was my job to make sure that it, along with all the other core brand recipes, was executed exactly the same way all over the globe. Sounds easy, right? It's a recipe: just follow it and it will be the same. *Yeah... nope.* Turns out that it's way more complicated than that. Just finding a mayonnaise that had the right flavor profile took dozens of hours to source in each foreign market. Have you ever done a mayonnaise tasting? Can I tell you how totally different mayonnaises can be? One is sweeter, one is creamier, one is greasier, one is more acidic, one is thicker, one is runnier... and on and on. If you use the wrong one, it throws off the whole recipe, and then you have to rebalance that difference somewhere else, through the other savory or acidic ingredients.

The same process was required with the curry powder blends available in the different global regions: one had more cumin, another had more chili, one had star anise with no fennel, another had fennel but no star anise, one was saltier, another spicier... the differences were endless. I came to know this particular recipe's flavor profile like the back of my hand because I spent so much time recreating it all over the world. I was trained by the original creator of the recipe, so I knew I had her blessing and that she trusted my palate and sensibilities. It's a difficult thing to have such an intangible deliverable, because it could easily be reasonable to say, "It's just Renee's opinion... it's what she likes, not actually 'the brand.'" I had to be completely confident that what I understood a given product to be was exactly correct so that I could replicate it everywhere else. So, it's not a stretch to imagine that

I could immediately recognize when the recipe was not being made "to spec" in my own backyard—in the good old U.S. of A.

What happened here? Suddenly, this turkey curry was *boring*. The correct, original recipe was refreshing and a total delight to eat. *That was not this*. I immediately got in touch with the team leader responsible. Typically, when something like this happened, either I or someone on my team would go to the facility and work side by side with the team there to diagnose and correct. But this manager was curiously unreceptive to exploring what might have gone wrong.

I flagged it with my boss and thought to myself, *Okay, maybe it was just the one batch*. But, really, in my view (back then and still now), even only one bad batch should never be let out into the business—it should be pulled from the shelves. When the customer experience is not up to par, it's an unacceptable breach of trust, and it damages your credibility. And this, as it turns out, was not just one bad batch. The next day, and the next brought the same dull, out-of-balance food experience.

I'll spare you the details, but it became a really contentious issue between the teams, and despite crazy efforts, it was never fully resolved. The executives did not want to get involved—in fact, they were mostly annoyed that my team was making it an issue at all. I couldn't get my head around it. If I looked at the Management Big Five, from where I was sitting, I was a complete failure. The business was compromised by this recipe change; the teams were damaged by what became toxic friction; the customers could no longer rely on the dish they loved and looked forward to; my bosses were pissed off because I was like a dog with a bone; and I personally was in turmoil over not being able to solve it all—it felt like a personal stain on my professional abilities. And without executive intervention, I was powerless.

Necessary Tension and Leadership Lecithin

When you're first starting out, it's easy to look ahead to your future in management and think, *That's when I will be able to do everything my way*. But there's a factor you might not be considering: conflict between your priorities and even between you and your fellow managers. Let's just say it like it is: Relationships between people in a business—those at the same level, and those above and below each other—can be *tense*. Yes, sometimes it comes down to personality, ways of communicating, differing leadership styles. But it's more than that, too. You each have your own spheres of responsibility, especially if you work in different business areas (procurement, sales, operations, legal, DEI & Talent), and you each have your own deliverables and goals. And they're not always in sync.

But that tension—between people, between priorities—doesn't have to be negative. There's a kind of energy that can occur when people with differing expertise and areas of focus come together to problem-solve, make decisions, and execute. It's challenging, frustrating, often unavoidable, and sometimes absolutely necessary in order to get the best results.

Proven, successful leaders will seek to find a healthy balance of tension between the different demands of their business because without it, there is no pressure to find the best possible outcome between all of the players involved. Basically, tension inspires response *because* it is uncomfortable. And tension can create a strong human desire for action.

But when that tension isn't healthy? It's *destructive*. I mean, really toxic. I have seen and experienced company cultures so cutthroat you'd think people were playing the Hunger Games. Bad behavior, politics, one-upmanship, dirty tricks, liars, suck-ups, suck-downs, suck-acrosses (can you even say that?) . . . you name it, I've seen it. Frankly, anyone who reaches the upper levels of management, in this industry or in any industry, will see it, too. Including you.

So, here's the trick: You have to learn to understand the difference between supporting toxic behaviors and supporting healthy tension. One is destructive to your career and those around you. One is necessary friction—an energy that drives performance. *Good friction*, if you will.

In the mysterious case of the turkey curry whodunit, I felt a duty to the business, the customers, and the brand to get it right. That was, after all, my job, and I cared a lot about the responsibility of being a standard bearer. While the burden felt enormously heavy in moments like that, I felt honored to be a champion of something so precious. I did not yet understand that my personal and professional values around quality were not always going to be the same as those of others—and I definitely didn't understand the value of letting something go . . . *yet.*

This is where mayonnaise comes back into the conversation. Love it or hate it, you have to respect the fact that mayo, or any sort of culinary emulsion, exists at all. To be able to take ingredients that don't combine permanently, like oil and vinegar, and then successfully mix them together with the help of an emulsifier is the ultimate metaphor for this phase of your career. Without getting all "chemistry" on you, chefs make this kind of magic happen all the time. I smile so much just imagining the obsession and grit that some culinary genius had way, way, back in order to spend days, if not years, finding a way to combine oil and vinegar with egg yolks to make a rich, silky, scrumptious sauce. As you work longer in the food world, you will understand (if you don't already) the incredible importance of making a really good mayo. And you will also learn that if you simply take the key ingredients—the aforementioned oil and vinegar—and then pour them into a bowl, they won't mix. *At all.* Even if you used a commercial grade emulsion blender (lovingly referred to by some culinary folks as a "Rambo"), these two ingredients will eventually separate, with the little oil globules just floating around in the vinegar.

But when you add in some egg yolk? *Watch out.* The lecithin found in the yolk acts as the binder that can hold the mixture together to become a perfectly formed, thick and luxurious sauce, permanently. *Emulsifier. Lecithin.* This is the surprisingly great uniter of ingredients that would otherwise be impossible to combine. Same for mustard seeds, by the way—another emulsifier. Does it sound like I am suggesting you become some kind of hokey "leadership lecithin" or "management mustard" if you want career success? *You bet your ass I am.*

As you move up the management ladder, your objective should be to learn how to strike the right balance between all of the responsibilities you hold—Management Big Five, baby!—and to bring people with different goals, objectives, and priorities together. To unite. *To emulsify.* To find solutions and not create more problems. To see the opportunity in good, necessary tension and recognize the energy and momentum it brings to the table in order to aid in the unification of all those competing priorities and opposing viewpoints. *To be glorious mayonnaise.* Not to separate and divide, like a hollandaise gone wrong. Trust me when I say that your dream career trajectory depends on it.

Remember when I said that your success will be driven more by your relationships than by your skills? The ability to create—no, *to be*—that lecithin is the absolute key to those relationships. I didn't understand this at all when I was first starting out. I thought that my performance would be measured by accuracy, results, and getting the job done well—it took me a long time to learn that this is only part of the equation. But I came to realize, by hard knocks, that great performance as a manager is not about doing the job perfectly or even correctly sometimes; rather, it is about how you can navigate and achieve the business objectives with all the personalities and opinions around you, especially when they differ from your own.

Back to the turkey curry conundrum. Somewhere in the midst of it all, the other team leader and I got paired up to open a new foreign market together. *Yikes.*

Me: Rigid, quality-minding pain in the ass.
Team leader: Lazy, recipe-ruining shortcutter.
Let's do this.

The introduction of the brand to this new market was such a success that, on a subsequent visit, the local leaders ended up looking into buying another restaurant chain that was for sale in a nearby region. It would be a fast way to add another dozen or so restaurants to the business and get even more brand visibility. So, we all clambered onto an overnight train, ready to tour the next day, and then jump right back on the train to the primary market the following afternoon.

On the outbound trip, several of us stayed up for a late dinner in the bar car. We were starving, exhausted, and jet-lagged, which was a common state back in those days. We had a member of the executive team traveling with us, along with the local leadership and some of their senior managers, and several translators. I don't know if it was the exhaustion, the wine, or the surreal nature of hanging out on an overnight train rolling through a faraway country, but a few of us decided it would be absolutely hilarious to take a picture of my "recipe ruining" nemesis and me snuggled up together in fake sleep in one of the sleeper cabins and send it to our teams. We knew their eyeballs would explode out of their heads, so, of course, we had to do it.

I remember resting my head in the nook of his arm and feeling his fuzzy winter sweater tickling the side of my cheek and thinking it was just unbelievable to be doing this after everything that had happened. It was so preposterous and childish and I could not stop laughing at the absurdity of it all. But can I just tell you that in that utterly ridiculous and unbelievable moment, we broke through the bad feelings we had between us and were able to move our relationship forward in a different, more productive way. It might sound a little nuts, but we found we had something in common—a wicked and childish sense of humor. And that shared joy of irreverence became the emulsifying agent that held our opposing perspectives together. *We had finally made some mayonnaise!*

From the perspective of the Management Big Five, things were looking up. But the pathway to success wasn't yet clear. Too many questions still remained and things were still too far out of balance. How were the customers handling the unexpected recipe change? How was my career doing? What kind of senior leadership chatter was happening about this problem and my inability to lead our collective teams to success? Was I becoming known as a rigid pain in the ass for quality? And was that a bad thing or a good thing? (It was my job, after all.) Had my midnight train hijinks undermined my professional credibility? *Time would tell.*

Discovering the Joys of Letting Go

About a month or so after that train trip, I got called into a meeting with one of the executives, a person who rarely used direct communication, so I was curious about why I was being summoned. You can imagine my surprise when he congratulated me on turning the page in that particularly frosty relationship—he called it something like "the unexpected success story of the year." *Yep, he's for sure seen the train picture,* I thought. I also thought, *But wait, I am actually failing because we haven't, in fact, solved the recipe problem!* It took all of my might to keep my mouth shut, honestly.

"Leadership Lecithin" Mayonnaise

ALL IN TAKES ABOUT 10 MINUTES • ACTIVE TIME 10 MINUTES

MAKES 1 HEAPING CUP

There are so many variations to this! You can use pretty much any vinegar or oil in combination, and it's also the perfect base for additions like fresh pesto and any other kind of aioli you want to make (garlic, roasted pepper, chipotle, rémoulade—you can just go to town). And here's a chef secret: sometimes I strain frying oil and use that for extra sneaky flavor. It's really all about feeling free to play around and practice. So feel free!

And yes, you can do this with an immersion blender if you combine everything except the oil, blend well, and add oil slowly to finish. A food processor works, too.

---

2 egg yolks, room temperature if possible

1 tablespoon Dijon mustard

1 cup oil *your choice—sunflower oil is my go-to*

2 to 3 teaspoons *either* fresh lemon juice or white wine vinegar

Maldon salt to your taste

Optional: black pepper to your taste

Whisk yolks and mustard together in a bowl. Slowly add a touch of the oil and whisk well to incorporate. Repeat for a couple of additions to make sure the mayo is emulsifying well.

Finish with a slow, gentle stream of oil while whisking. *Yes, your arm will hurt, but it's worth it, so keep going.*

Once all of the oil has been added, start with 2 teaspoons of the lemon juice or vinegar and whisk to incorporate. Season with Maldon salt and your pepper, if desired. Add more lemon juice or vinegar if you want more zing. *You're the boss, after all!*

Store in the fridge for up to 3 days.

I understood why that executive felt things were now on a good trajectory. From his view, there was no more debate or obvious conflict, so everything was golden. But from my view, he was dead wrong. The recipe had lost its special unique characteristics (in other words, it sucked) and by now the "flat" version had become the new normal. Frankly, I was mystified by the praise, but no one else seemed to care at all. For younger-manager me, the realization that the soul of the food was clearly not a priority to leadership was *devastating*.

Then, as I was hashing out the situation with one of my treasured, straight-talking PBOD mentors, he hit me over the head with the reality of the situation. None of this had anything to do with recipe accuracy, brand standard reinforcement, or how I did my job. It had everything to do with how the senior folks *perceived* me. It was about my reputation and how I measured up, and whether or not I was easy to work with, a team player, and not "stirring up trouble." So, in that moment, my career was in a good spot entirely because I had some drinks, made some jokes, and took some funny pictures. *Huh?*

Realizing that achieving the goals and targets that leadership had set out for me was not the ultimate measure of my career success was a game changer. I mean, don't get me wrong: the executive teams I worked for did care about results and targets, and it helped a lot that I consistently met them. But there was way more to the story. In those years, I remember vividly oscillating between feeling like a "good," valued employee and feeling conflicted and confused much of the time. As I became a more skilled and capable professional, I was also becoming a wiser, more emotionally mature *human*. Management was revealing itself to be full of rich learnings, new experiences, exposure to leaders with the greatest skill sets and strategic thinking, and tons of exercise for my resilience muscle (all that "responsibility without authority"). I tried to focus on those aspects of the roles that were inspiring and personally motivating to me while I quietly reflected on the things that felt hard and that I wanted to change. I was growing older, and my goals and priorities for my personal life were changing. What I needed, I realized, was the opportunity for more joy in my day-to-day. Remember that fifth "flavor" of the Management Big Five? *The needs of yourself?*

I can give full credit to turkey curry for this awakening. It was so odd to be jolted into this new kind of reality because I had never had that kind of thinking on my radar before. But as I progressed in my career, changed jobs, got promoted, switched companies, and moved forward again, I came to understand why the executives in my earlier years valued collaborative relationships over things like accuracy and quality. It was my job as a manager to bring forward challenges and provide solutions. It was *their* job to greenlight those solutions or not. And if they didn't? I could just let it go.

Wait, what? Let it go? Won't my career be stained for eternity if I don't solve every problem I encounter? Actually, nope. When you hit this moment of realization in your own management career—and you will—you can exhale deeply and understand that once you have delivered the solution, you can lay that burden on the doorstep of your leaders and then move on with your life, feeling light and free. I don't call it the "joy" of letting go for nothing!

If it hadn't been for the excellent coaching I received from my PBOD, I would have screwed this up royally and stunted my own career growth by continuing the fight. I couldn't see the value anyone would have in not doing something absolutely correctly. But hear me now: Finding a way to balance the Management Big Five so that those elements are mostly in harmony is the secret to moving forward in your career. From the view of your senior leadership, *perception is everything.* So quit burning your hands on that hot potato and pass it on to someone else. This particular place in your career journey is one of the few times when you'll be able to do that, so enjoy it while it lasts!

In fact, discovering the joy of letting go can release an entirely different way of being a professional. Working with passion and abandon and understanding how you personally balance *all* of the Management Big Five—not just achieving targets—is actually your personal measure for success as well. Depending on what your particular organization and its leadership value the most—whether that's hitting financial targets, or positive feedback about your work from others, or bringing big ideas to the table—you can intuitively begin to shift and move each of the five important pillars like levers toward your collective success.

And as you learn more about what those values are, you can also use that information to assess what you personally care about and whether or not that organization is a good fit for you. As you can imagine, in that turkey curry instance, I soon realized it was time to find a role in a different organization that aligned better with my values, and where I could have the autonomy to lead, develop, and deploy strategy, and pursue new product ideas and innovation closer to my own standards.

It's Not Just You

The most important thing to remember as you slowly uncover your own balance of the Management Big Five is that *you are not alone.* I went through it. Your own leaders went through it. Pretty much every colleague I know went through it and has taken those experiences and important learning lessons with them as they moved up the ladder. The challenges you will face as you find yourself—as a manager, a colleague, a person with unique values—are how you will learn to negotiate complex, dynamic relationships and balance those delicate, critical, and often conflicting priorities.

Yes, it's a time that can feel confusing and sometimes even excruciating. But trust me when I tell you that it is all so incredibly valuable as you continue further into your leadership journey. These are the years in which you are truly going to "grow up" as a professional. You will make a lot of mistakes and get many opportunities, and you will craft out of them a toolkit full of hard-earned skills and knowledge. So, once again, lean into that resilience muscle—it's getting so strong by now!—and keep moving forward. There is so much waiting for you on the other side.

TIME TO GET INTO MISE MODE

Your prep for learning to balance your business, your bosses, your customers, your team, and your own unignorable needs.

MINDSET SHIFT: You may think an issue is pressing and obvious, but your bosses and executives may not have the same priorities you do! Pay attention and learn about what matters *to them* so that you can realign the Management Big Five levers and deliver what matters most in their eyes.

TRADE SECRET: "See something, say something"—but not on the first day! Things may be as they are for a reason, so as you enter an environment as a new manager, take ample time to observe, listen, assess, and understand. Keep your Pocket List handy for your thoughts and ideas—you can put them into action once you fully know how the game is being played.

LEADERSHIP LOWDOWN: Lecithin is the yolky magic that turns oil and water into delicious mayonnaise. Everyone you work with at every level is going to have different priorities and different goals. If you can be the emulsifier that unites those agendas, that's going to take you further than any knife skills or business ideas ever could.

INSIDER DISH

Amazing career insights and so much more ... this way!

9

THE REAL BREAD AND BUTTER
Understanding Fiduciary Duty

When in doubt—
go business first.

OOOOOOH, we get to talk numbers now! The nerd in me is literally rubbing her hands together with anticipation! So let's start at the beginning. Wherever you land in management—whether it's in a creative role, a service role, or an operations role—you will have a professional responsibility to look out for the needs of the business as you execute, problem-solve, and guide your teams in the day-to-day work of accomplishing your collective goals. Lecithin and mayo talk aside, the bottom line is the bottom line.

When I was first starting out, there was never a word or phrase that described the instinct I felt to protect the businesses and teams I was responsible for. I knew I had to carry out my duties and lead others to do the same, but how did those duties relate to the overall success of the business? And what was this "protect the business" instinct called? "Fiduciary duty" is pretty close, but it's a legal term and it doesn't encompass the whole range of responsibilities you will have to look out for. So I like to call it the Bread-and-Butter Principle.

Basically, you have been anointed in your management role with protecting the interests of the business, and you are expected to meet the financial targets and goals you committed to delivering when you accepted the job. This means that not only are you an agent for the business, but you also *represent* the company that employs you. This includes ensuring that the doors open on time, that the business is correctly staffed to both the budget and operational needs, and that your teams understand their duties and responsibilities and carry them out as needed.

As a manager, you will need to hold this perspective in the background at all times—when you are dealing with your staff, customers, budgets, operations . . . everything you do all day. It's like breathing. You don't consciously think about it—you need it, and it just happens. That's how automated the Bread-and-Butter Principle will have to become for you as you use your problem-solving consciousness.

The expression "bread and butter," if you're not familiar, means the economic foundation on which something stands—your best-seller, for example. A chef might say, "Our roast chicken is our bread-and-butter dish." It's where you make your living. *It's how your bread gets buttered.* In order to be able to offer you a paid job, the company that employs you has to perform well. A seasoned manager will understand that their decisions and how they achieve their targets directly impacts the company's overall performance. If that performance is poor and targets aren't met, then perks disappear, folks start to lose jobs, hours get cut, and other hard decisions get made to keep the company viable until the performance is better. It's that simple. Company does well, salaries, perks, and benefits happen. Company does poorly, it has to pay its costs somehow, and everything is on the table, including and especially jobs. That's where you come in, and that's why your performance matters so much.

One of the greatest gifts of looking at your career through the lens of the Management Big Five is understanding what putting *business first* can unlock in your career journey. Think of those beer tap handles I described for you in the last chapter—leaning on the one marked "business" when you aren't sure what to do in a given moment can be an excellent way to get through sticky situations and guide your team to success. *When in doubt—go business first.*

This topic—business first—has come up so many times over the course of my career that it needs its own chapter. Because, curiously, the "why" of the business is not often discussed between managers and bosses. There is an odd disconnect that seems to happen regularly within businesses: senior leaders expect managers to intuitively understand why the business matters and especially how it's all connected to their personal performance, yet neglect to start that actual conversation about why the targets are what they are and why they matter at all. It's a completely untapped area of energy and motivation that you personally can grab on to and bring to your team. The excellent engagement you can drive by taking the time to explain the "whys" to your team is powerful beyond words.

Numbers and Targets and Sales, Oh My!

Here's how it breaks down: Your senior leadership is responsible for setting out a clear road map to what success looks like. Your professional responsibility is to take that road map and deliver the results. And that starts with your annual budgets. *Budgets, baby!* It's really important to know where the business is headed, so that the right levels of staffing are in place, the right amount of ingredients and supplies are purchased, and the team knows exactly what they need to do to "bring home the bacon." Budgets are a big deal because they become the day-by-day blueprint to achieving the goals for the whole year.

I remember being handed my first weekly budget as a new manager and wondering how the numbers were determined, and how on earth I could personally influence the results. Oddly, no one ever sat me down and explained to me how that budget came to exist and what would happen if it got off track day-to-day. I watched as some of my colleagues took those numbers, added the daily sales and costs "because the boss said to," then set them aside as the busyness of the day called away their attention. The end result? They never had the time to figure out what those numbers meant. Worse, many of those folks didn't feel comfortable asking questions because they thought they were just supposed to know and didn't want to seem incompetent or dumb. I was lucky because I had a boss who invested time in explaining to me how the numbers came to be—that person ignited a true curiosity and passion within me to figure to how to make the numbers happen and hit my budget. Hey, I'm a competitive middle child. I was all in to beat those numbers and win!

So, what is the "why" I learned about? A well-planned weekly budget will include daily sales targets, daily cost targets for goods and labor, and even a place where you can record information about that particular day. (Was it a holiday? Sunshine or rain? Were there special orders? Anything odd happening in the news or in the local area that might impact sales?) All of this information matters because it helps your accounting team and leadership continuously refine future budgets and understand and plan for the normal ebbs and flows of the business.

Basically, a team of financial wizards will "roll up" all of this information, and when it comes time to do budgets for the next year, it will all be considered and included as the financial plan gets developed. Look at it this way: Day-to-day sales become weeks, which become months, which become quarters, which become the full year. Breaking down the annual goals into daily goals helps the local teams tasked with delivering those results to stay on track. *Here's what you have to do this week, broken down by day.* That's a lot easier to achieve than being handed a full-year budget and being told, "Go get 'em, tiger!" What would you be able to do with that?

But wait, there's more! Budgets also go hand in hand with a strategy to make them achievable and also allow them to stretch into new levels of growth. Healthy businesses want to be able to demonstrate a steady rate of sales growth each year to show they are strong and viable. This rate of growth becomes a number called a "comp," or a "comparable sale," or even "same-store sales," where the retail or restaurant business revenue for a particular period gets compared to a similar period and/or location.

What the heck does that even mean? I'm so glad you asked!

You want your comps to be positive because that's the number that indicates growth. For example, "Last year, this second week of May, I brought in $10,000 in sales, and this same week this year, I brought in $12,000, so my comp for this week is 20 percent, same period, year to year (*in other words, kick-ass amazing!*)." Or, "Last year in this third week of August, I sold $10,000, and this same week this year, I only sold $9,000, so my comp is down 10 percent, same period, year to year (*in other words, oh shit, better get back on track*)."

In case you're as curious as I was (*thanks, ninth-grade algebra!*), here is the actual formula to figure out a comp. The important thing is to make sure you are comparing apples to apples in your time period: so, week to week, month to month, day to day, or year to year.

$$\text{Comp Sales} = ((X-Y) \div Y) \times 100$$
$$X = \textit{Current Sales}$$
$$Y = \textit{Previous Period Sales}$$

To give you a little more perspective, McDonald's had a staggering same-store-sales comp of 13.8 percent in the US in 2021, which was their highest comp ever reported. A 13.8 percent increase in growth year over year! *Holy comp!* Their global systemwide sales reached $112.5 billion that year. Yes, *billion*, with a *B*. That's a lot of cheeseburgers. Because they are a publicly traded company, and people like you and me can invest in them by purchasing shares, they have to report their financials every three months.

Comp sales are a pivotal part of demonstrating the current strength of their business—*their value.* It means people are eating at McDonald's way more than ever before, so it might be worth investing in . . . if, that is, you can get past the outrageously low wages they pay most of their workforce and their destructive impact on human, animal, and environmental health. To be clear, I'm not trying to pick on McDonald's—I *love* their french fries—but seriously, with a reported $7.5 billion in profit in the US alone for 2021, it's kind of a reasonable assumption that they could do a lot better, a lot faster, on all fronts. *Mickey D's—I am rooting for you to create some much better impacts! (Yes, this is shameless, opportunistic, old-school peer pressure.)* But anyhoo—let's stay focused on the numbers that matter to you.

Once you begin to understand the "whys" of your business targets and goals and the importance of the Bread-and-Butter Principle, you can bring those "whys" to your team to empower them to buy in. Thing is, the folks who make these results happen are in fact the team members on the front lines. The folks with boots on the ground. *You and your team.* Your personal performance as a manager and that of your team are critical to the business achieving its overall goals. A strong manager is regularly looking at a bunch of different metrics so they can get a broad view of the business and where opportunities may exist (comps are just one of many!). That's why those numbers on those pages really matter, and not just to your bosses, but to you and your career.

Harness the Power of Your Team to Connect the Dots

Think back for a moment to that story I told you in chapter 3 about how I got tapped on the shoulder as a younger manager to move back to Europe. I was tasked with all sorts of goals, like pulling together an updated food and beverage offering, launching a dinner service, upgrading recipes, and conducting a full ingredient review including cost and quality, as well as optimizing back-of-the-house (kitchen) operations. Oh, and I was also supposed to increase the overall sales each week in each of the locations. *You know, just your garden-variety targets. Ha!* I was so excited and motivated by all the opportunity, but I was also still finding my way as a manager. Suddenly, I was working in another country and language, with a team of people who were wondering why I was there and what I was going to ask them to do, and I had only twelve weeks to understand the dynamics, assess the business, determine the changes needed, make a plan, get the team on board, and drive the behavioral and operational changes for long-term success. No problem, right? *Gah!*

Upon arrival, I immediately saw that the teams were unfocused, disorganized, and struggling with a lack of direction. They didn't seem to have a sense of urgency at all around meeting their objectives. Most didn't know what their objectives even were, and it was all just so bizarre and unexpected that I felt like I was in a restaurant management Twilight Zone. Remember "Le Gros Fromage"? It seemed so strange to me that he had such deep concerns about the performance of this critical market for the brand, yet the actual team on the ground had barely a care in the world. Talk about a disconnect!

I knew that if I was going to be impactful, I would have to invest in key relationships and earn the respect I needed to help change behaviors. I was going to have to connect the dots between the team behaviors and the gaps in company performance. So, I dug in and basically lived in the restaurants for the first several weeks, getting to know the teams and operations and working side by side as much as I could. "Le Gros Fromage" had positioned this project as an opportunity for me to demonstrate my abilities, so I knew that my career path was on the line. *If this goes sideways, so will my job,* I thought. The stakes felt extremely high, and I felt so visible and exposed, with an actual executive personally overseeing my results across the entire project. The pressure was enormous. I had to deliver. No other option.

I quickly discovered that one of the biggest challenges the team had was "turning the tables"—getting customers to eat and leave within a reasonable time frame so you can fill that table again but doing it in a way that never makes anyone feel rushed. Getting that balance right is absolutely critical to creating a positive customer experience while maximizing sales. It takes two ingredients to pull this off—finesse and a workforce all on the same page—and we seemed to have neither. Saturdays and Sundays were the big moneymakers and a gorgeous brunch menu was the hook. But people were staying for *hours.* Imagine a table of six tied up for three hours while lines of people waited in frustration out the door. Meanwhile, the waitstaff were unbothered. They hadn't yet made the connection between the snail's pace they kept when serving and the subsequent lack of sales.

I remember watching one server take an order from a large table, walk over and put it into the system, and then sit down for a smoke break at a table directly across from the customers. *Sitting with friends! In the middle of their shift!* And the manager seemed fine with all of it. *WTF!* That's when I knew we had a major cultural issue to tackle.

Don't get me wrong: it's entirely possible to support the enjoyment of life and still maintain a culture in which the entire team is motivated to support the success of the business. *Bread and butter, baby!* Where did this team think their paychecks came from? In order to influence behaviors and drive the changes required for success, I needed to get them to buy in. That meant I had to demonstrate *why* these changes were needed and *why* the team would personally benefit from making them. I basically had to convince each person that they needed to work harder, do more, move faster, and behave more professionally. I needed to help them connect the dots between the health of the business and their own personal success.

If I went about this the wrong way, they were going to think I was crazy, resulting in nothing more than them hating my guts and everything staying the same. I was leaving in twelve weeks, after all, so they had the option to ignore me as they waited for the clock to tick down. So how did I pull it off? By leaning on three of the central tenets of successful workforce engagement: *acknowledgment, recognition, and reward.* At the time, I didn't even know this was a thing, and it was so wild to discover in later years that the methods I had been deploying were actual legit business strategies! *Thanks again, PBOD!*

Each time you step up or over into a new role with new responsibilities, you are going to face unfamiliar challenges and unexpected obstacles all over the place, just like I did as younger-manager me. That's totally normal—in fact, that's actually the job! But the secret to success is not about one person's performance or ability to identify challenges and offer solutions. The most significant asset in any business is its workforce. Its employees. *Its people.*

I could have offered up ideas about how to solve the problems for that business all day long. But if I couldn't earn the team's trust and inspire behavioral changes, all those great ideas would have failed because no one would have executed them. It's that simple. As a manager—as a *coach and guide*—no matter how large or small your team, the more investment you personally make in their evolution into more skilled and capable employees, and the more time you spend deepening their understanding of the financial side of the business, the better for all of you. It will support your success as a manager; their success as competent, valued, and experienced employees; and the business's success as an organization that fosters a dynamic and talented team achieving awesome and satisfying results. *Everybody profits!*

In the end, I was able to win over that team by working alongside them to help them learn the new techniques and strategies, thoroughly explaining the "whys," and showing them what the results would be if they decided to make the effort. Thankfully, after a short while, they were so energized to be part of the changes—especially as they saw the results improve—that they started bringing in their own ideas for boosting sales and opening up profits. I even got invited to a team member's home for a celebration-turned-strategy session (she got a well-deserved promotion) that included the most incredible tartiflette of my life. *I mean, what genius decided to layer paper-thin slices of potatoes with cream, onions, garlic, white wine, lardons (tiny strips of browned bacon) and Reblochon cheese in a heavy pan, and then pop it in the oven until perfectly melted?* You're not living if you haven't had one. Next-level, unmatchable, unbeatable, other-worldly indulgence.

Truth be told, this assignment was one of the most challenging experiences of my professional life, and it definitely was not all roses—not even close. But it was extremely rewarding to see all of that gorgeous momentum building day by day, and I consider it one of the most impactful experiences I have had to date in my career. It's where I realized the full power of storytelling, coaching, and taking the time needed to listen and observe, and then educate and explain. The lessons learned were so rich and Herculean that they informed my work in all the years ahead—and now they are informing yours, too. *Bread and butter, baby!*

Discipline Is the Not-So-Secret Secret Ingredient of Success

Imagine you're a warehouse assistant manager and you're heading into the building to start your day. It's a little before 6 a.m. and you're early because you have a lot of time-sensitive tasks to accomplish, including finalizing next month's schedule and submitting your P&L (profit and loss statement) to the finance team for the weekly numbers rollup, which is due at 8 a.m. You also have an important client walkthrough and an inspection of the facilities booked for 9 a.m.—if you can help land that account, there will be a ton of new business coming in. After that, you have a DEI & Talent team meeting with an employee who missed her shift yesterday, and not for the first time.

As you walk in the door, a forklift operator drops a pallet of flour right in front of you, which sends teeny flecks of white powder everywhere. *So. Much. Flour.* As you rush over to make sure no one is hurt, you hear a loud rumble from the loading dock—one of the drivers has crashed their truck into a concrete loading bay, denting the truck badly and damaging its mechanical loading platform. There are no injuries from either accident, but now you have to arrange for urgent repairs and cleanup on top of everything else. How do you prioritize your efforts in order to accomplish all these deliverables and any other unplanned challenges that will crop up before the end of your day? It's only 6 a.m.!

This kind of scenario happens every day in the food world, so you will need to master the art of being disciplined about what to focus on and where to spend your energy for maximum efficiency as the work becomes more complex and you start to get pulled in a million different directions. Knowing what your goals and targets are and then mapping out ways to achieve them is how you start—and then you keep referring to that plan, as if it were a personal compass.

A lot of new managers get buried in the weeds of day-to-day fire-fighting and lose sight of the big-picture goals they are tasked with accomplishing. On any given day, lots of things will arise that you didn't anticipate. Many of these issues will seem urgent in the moment, and you will feel pressured to solve them immediately, but when you stand back, you might see that some are not so time sensitive after all. This is where smart multitasking comes into play.

Strong leaders learn to identify their priorities and keep them front and center. Let's say your target for labor costs is 22 percent of your weekly budget. If you keep your awareness on that, you will be less inclined to approve excess overtime and instead find ways for everyone to work more efficiently. So, when Jane runs into your office at the end of her shift and says that the kitchen is behind in peeling potatoes for the roasted garlic herbed mash needed for that night's special and offers to stay and take care of it, you don't mindlessly agree and carry on with your paperwork. Instead, you find another way to get that job done, even if it means rolling up your sleeves and grabbing a peeler yourself. Because . . . target!

If you don't know your goal, then you might approve that overtime without realizing that you are jeopardizing your target as well as the company's profits. I mean, it's just a little overtime, right?

Nope. It never is.

Every decision has a consequence, some intended and obvious, some not. Being disciplined will help you make good decisions and stay focused on what really matters.

And if you want to know how I would prioritize those issues in the flour-bomb-accident scenario, it would be like this: keep the P&L

deadline and client meeting on track; push the DEI & Talent team meeting to late in the day; be present and available for the team as they go through the accident paperwork (auto, warehouse, forklift); make an assessment about how the accidents occurred and remedy anything immediately needing attention (safety first—always); ensure any necessary worker's comp filings are executed; make sure the employees involved are interviewed and those interviews are documented; contact the insurers to put them on notice. I would also brew a fresh pot of coffee for everyone and pull a team member or two off non-urgent duties to support cleanup and getting the warehouse in shape before the client arrives at 9 a.m. (and to ensure that no further accidents are created *from* the initial ones). Later on, I would circle back with the team members involved to double-check for any injuries that show up later in the day—sometimes it takes a few hours or even more for these to surface. I would add myself to the agenda of the coming days' shift meetings to talk about safety and learn more about what I could do to help the team avoid these kinds of preventable accidents moving forward, and then schedule retraining as needed. You know: take the learnings, make necessary adjustments, support, retrain, and optimize. (This won't be the last you hear about learning and optimizing... just wait until the next chapter.)

Boil It Down: Communicate Like a Leader

Perhaps now you can understand the importance of communication in management and why style and messaging matters so much when it comes to educating your teams, creating buy-in, and ultimately hitting your goals. In fact, how you communicate the "whys" to your team will be an important indicator of your own personal ability to lead. The tone of voice you use, the words you choose, the way you consider your audience as you frame your message—it all points to your leadership style, and it will all drive the outcome. Why? Because of *connection and relatability.* Think about it: Are you more likely to work your ass off for someone you like, admire, respect, and connect with, or someone who shouts orders, makes no attempt to know you, and then disappears? *Option A for me, please.*

"If They Can't Peel Then I Will, 'Cuz Budget!" Roasted Garlic Herbed Mash

ALL IN TAKES ABOUT 75 MINUTES • ACTIVE TIME 20 TO 25 MINUTES

MAKES 4 TO 6 GENEROUS PORTIONS, PLUS SOME EXTRA

Here's a mom tip: Take any leftover mash, place it directly on a sheet of aluminum foil, wrap it tightly to seal, and throw it in the fridge. It becomes a valuable side dish for another meal later in the week (with a toddler at home, I save anything I can reheat easily; plus, I hate wasting food, so we are a household big on leftovers). When I want to use the mash in a meal, I just throw it in the oven, turn the oven on to 350°F, and voilà! About 30 minutes later, hot and delicious mash and no cleanup.

If you don't like garlic or want to switch it up, try adding a heap of grated Parmigiano-Reggiano instead. Or use sour cream and chives instead of parsley. Or try it with grated aged cheddar, crumbled warm bacon, and chopped scallions!

Cheffy tip: You can make this well in advance of your meal (2+ hours) if you hold it over a bain-marie (double boiler). Fill a saucepot about a quarter full with water, set a snug-fitting stainless-steel bowl over the top, and set it on low heat. Place the mash in the bowl on top before you add the herbs or finish seasoning, then hold, covered tightly in plastic wrap, until ready to serve. Finish by adding the herbs and seasoning just before serving. Good to go!

---

2 whole heads garlic

2½ to 3 pounds mashing potatoes Yukon Gold, russet, or whatever your farmer recommends.

1 to 1½ cups organic whole milk

8 to 12 ounces + 2 pats unsalted butter, at room temperature if possible

1 cup fresh Italian parsley, stems removed and chopped fine

Maldon salt and ground white pepper, to your taste

Preheat oven to 375°F. The easiest way to prep garlic for roasting is to slice off the tops of the heads horizontally about a third of the way down to expose the very top of the cloves. Add a small pat of butter and a pinch of Maldon salt to the top of each head, then wrap each head tightly by placing it on top of a small square of aluminum foil and folding the foil up and over the top. *It will look like a pointy little gnome hat—do it this way to keep the melted butter inside. You don't want butter spilling in the oven because it will smoke and burn and become a major pain in your ass.* Place the heads directly on your oven rack and roast for about 1 hour.

Wash and peel the potatoes and place them directly into a saucepot with enough cold water to cover. Boil the potatoes gently until cooked through. Hold "off heat" on the stove until the roasted garlic is ready. *If the potatoes aren't uniform in size, cut them into similar-sized pieces so they cook evenly.*

Once the garlic is ready, remove it from the oven and gently peel back the aluminum foil to make sure it is soft and melty. Strain the potatoes, place them back in the pot, add the milk and butter, and then mash with a hand masher. *More milk = fluffier; more butter = heavier/ richer. (I usually go heavy on both.)*

Once at your preferred consistency, add the garlic by holding the aluminum foil package upside down over the mash and squeezing the cloves out from the base head directly into the mash. *Use an oven mitt or dish towel to protect your hands from the hot garlic.* Mash again to incorporate. Then either hold it here following the cheffy tip or finish it off with the final step!

When ready to serve, adjust the seasoning with Maldon and white pepper. Add the chopped herbs and mix with a large spoon to incorporate, and serve directly. *Don't be shy with the salt and pepper... you want them to be well seasoned!*

It's the same principle for how goals and targets get communicated. Just like with a good demi-glace, "boiling down" a message will make it much more memorable—and much more impactful. I still remember the amazement I felt in culinary school when I first learned that a demi-glace was the super-stealth sub-recipe that fed into every luxurious, rich, and gorgeous sauce I had been dying over. *Boiling it down made it exceptional.* It's the same for how you communicate to your team: smart, boiled-down storytelling is the stealth sub-recipe for motivating your team toward achievement.

Let's use finance as an example. Making a restaurant work financially is really not a mystery. You can't spend what you don't make—and if you do, that's when the trouble starts. It's the same principle used by a billion-dollar diet industry built on solving the eternal question everyone already knows the answer to—*calories in versus calories out.* It's literally that simple. But the complexity of all the ways and hows and whys one can or should manage their diet, or in this case, their business, makes the simple answer completely unfathomable.

If I were faced with an inventory-taking hater on my team, I would talk about perspective. Something like, "The process is a pain, for sure, but when you come up with missing inventory worth three thousand dollars at the end of the month, while that may seem like no big deal to you, I am looking at an entirely different number. We have thirty-six restaurants in this region, so imagine what three thousand dollars times thirty-six would look like. That's right, it's one hundred and eight thousand dollars a month—more than a million a year. Now *that* number feels worthy of attention, doesn't it?" *Calories in versus calories out.*

I've had to explain this again and again, probably thousands of times over the course of my management career, and each time, I could see the light bulb go off in the employee's mind—they would realize that each small action they took in their role day to day (portioning ingredients, managing overtime hours, and, yes, tracking inventory) all matters greatly to keeping the business under control. That's the connection: each employee personally has direct impact on the health of the business that also happens to pay their wages. *Money doesn't just fall out of the sky!* And healthy businesses create more career opportunities, right?

Boiling it down can also get folks on the same page. Take cleanliness, for example. The act of cleaning is one of the most important functions of the food world and can never be understated in significance. Having clean operations and cleaning with the right products *the right way* is critical to keeping people safe—both your employees and your customers. And as anyone who has ever shared a household with a spouse or a roommate knows, "clean" can mean very different things to different people.

One of my earliest bosses had worked at a fast-casual food chain where "Clean = Like New" was the informal verbal standard for cleaning. It was so basic and descriptive that everyone understood what cleanliness should look like. Genius! As soon as I started using that phrase to describe the standard I was looking for in my own workplaces, it closed any gaps in understanding within my teams—and the results were sparkling. I never forgot this solid advice and have trained with it ever since. If it doesn't look new, it's not clean. *Boom.*

Those light-bulb moments have been some of the richest and most rewarding experiences of my career—that is, helping others understand the business and buy into their deeply important part of it all. It felt so good to walk through the door of one of the restaurants I was responsible for and pass a team member who would proudly show off their cleaning efforts or give me a fist bump and say, "Calories in versus calories out, baby... I'm on it!" Those were the moments when I'd know we were in it together, charging forward in the same direction with the same goal: to get that good ol' bread and butter safely on the table.

TIME TO GET INTO MISE MODE

Your prep for teaching and executing your fiscal responsibility so you can keep serving up that critical bread and butter.

MINDSET SHIFT: Whether you see yourself on the creative side, the business side, or, really, *any* side as a manager, fiduciary duty is your key responsibility. *Calories in, calories out.* If that equation is off, then your business is in trouble.

TRADE SECRET: If the Management Big Five is a series of beer taps that you have to keep flowing, then the "needs of the business" is the go-to tap to pull on whenever you're unsure of what to prioritize. If the business isn't in a good place, then neither are your bosses, customers, or team—and neither are you.

LEADERSHIP LOWDOWN: If you want your team to understand your message, then do the work to make it understandable. Boil your message down to a simple principle that is easy to relate to—short, catchy, clear, and true. If they can relate to it, they can buy into it.

INSIDER DISH

You do not want to miss these insights!

10

ALWAYS FRESH, NEVER STALE

The Power of Staying in Growth Mode

We all make mistakes.
What we do with them
is what separates
the champions from the
almost-champions.

———————————————

IF I HAVEN'T DELIVERED THIS MESSAGE clearly enough yet, here it is in one sentence: it's safe to say that all the jobs (or at least almost all the jobs) you will have in your career will be very challenging. I can certainly say that every role I have ever held has been personally challenging, and each for very different reasons. But feeling challenged, in itself, is not a reason to be discouraged. In fact, feeling challenged is when you know you are in *growth mode.*

Growth mode is a beautiful thing, and it's a state you want to be in despite the difficulties that lie at the heart of its nature. Say you had a job where you already knew everything, met no new people, had no new interactions or experiences, and basically encountered no surprises or learnings, ever. You'd mastered it all and were essentially the ruler of the universe. Okay... by this point in the book, you have hopefully realized that this job doesn't exist. Or, if it does, something has gone seriously wrong, and you may have been abducted by aliens. Either way, I think we can move past this expectation. And that's the amazing part: moving past this expectation is actually a gift!

You will always be learning, you will always be having new experiences, and you will always be meeting new people and taking on new challenges and projects at work. *Always.* And if you aren't, it's because you aren't putting yourself into places where you can grow, which means no development is taking place in your professional life and you are stuck in a career black hole. (Hint: this is not good.)

Sure, if you don't want to take on more responsibilities and are happy where you are, doing what you are doing, that satisfaction is really important to recognize. And good for you! Maybe you don't want the difficulties and effort that come with more responsibility, or maybe your personal dream job lies in another profession. Lots of people work in the food world to support themselves while they focus on careers such as acting, writing, or photography.

But you've read this far, so I'm guessing that's not the full picture for you. This book is about moving forward in your career in the food industry and taking advantage of all the incredible opportunities, and I think that's what you want. So, to achieve your next steps, it's important for you to embrace growth mode and learn to stay in it. And it's also important to be able to pick apart feeling challenged from feeling unhappy, so you can make clear decisions at each point in your career about when to stay, when to leave, and why.

Your Career Garbage Is Valuable!

Bear with me as I use a bit of a "trashy" analogy here. In the food industry, there are so many ways to make money off your garbage. As a food professional, I have made it a practice to always pay attention to what's going in the garbage can because there is so much learning in what has been thrown away. You would be shocked by what you can discover about an operation from just looking in the trash. Food scraps can teach you how skilled the cooks are at prepping ingredients and minimizing waste. Spoiled products can teach you how good your team is at managing their inventory rotation and even accurately projecting demand. Basically, every single thing that goes into the trash in a food operation is like dollar bills getting dumped into the landfill. Some of those dollars can't be avoided and are precalculated into recipe yields (for example, the weight of the peels in a fifty-pound sack of potatoes you are ordering), but other trash will come from unplanned accidents, like burning an omelet or absentmindedly using sugar instead of salt in a large batch of Bolognese that no one tasted before they started making, like, twenty lasagnas. Sugary sweet, meaty dessert lasagne, anyone? All trash. Big money down the drain. A total waste. *Or is it?*

There is so much you can learn from these types of accidents after they happen. Taking the time to revisit the incident, diagnosing where it all went wrong, determining what process needs to be put in place to make sure it isn't repeated, and taking the learnings and making improvements are all strong, positive outcomes when the unexpected occurs. So, in that light, it seems obvious that there are valuable lessons in waste, right? And that means your own career "waste" is worth a lot as well.

I know it seems like one thing for a prep cook to waste ingredients, an office assistant to type in the wrong number on the purchase order for a produce delivery, or an apprentice brewer to spoil a tank of craft beer, and quite another for a manager to make a misstep that costs someone their job or the company hundreds of thousands of dollars. But in a strange way, it's not: the stakes feel higher, but the lessons are bigger, and the growth—if you handle it right—is exponential. Let me put it this way: When you experience accidents, bad decisions, or even epic, disastrous failures, will true recovery come from throwing those mistakes away, covering them up, and quickly moving on? Or will it come from owning them, fixing them, and finding ways to make sure they never happen again?

You know where I'm going with this. Everyone has accidents and makes mistakes. What you *do* with yours makes you either a champion or an almost-champion. You can make improvements to processes and projects continually throughout your management career by giving positive attention to that simple fact of life. *Trash is valuable. Mistakes are valuable.* If you can demonstrate to your team that you are good with mistakes and failures, then so long as lessons are learned, you are creating an environment in which people know they can risk failure in order to try new things and bring creativity and innovation to their work. And they can do it feeling comfortable in the trust that through it all, they will be supported by you. This is the kind of environment that eventually leads to big wins.

When it gets overwhelming and you feel like you're underwater—*and you will!*—that's when you hit that speed dial and call on your PBOD. Check in with the past and present leaders you respect the most, solicit their expert advice, and get a second opinion on your actions and thinking as you navigate all of this pressure-laden, unknown territory.

It's Time to Get Real with Yourself

This vulnerability applies not only when you've made mistakes, but also when you think you're in the right. Working with others and adapting to their way of seeing things is never easy and can sap a lot of energy out of you as you walk through the important journey of discovering your "manager self." But while it can be painful sometimes, man, is it awesome to see the positive impact other people—the mentors and the gossips, the high-performing folks and the "randy Jasons"—have on your personal and professional growth. They are a gift, all of them.

Every successful food company must constantly adapt to survive the shifts of consumer and cultural demands. If you don't innovate and grow your business, you're dead in the water. It's the same for "leadership you." Remember what I said in chapter 4 about seeing all feedback, no matter how painful, as an invaluable tool? This still applies when you reach the management level—in fact, more than ever. As you move into management, and eventually into the big leagues of being an executive, you have to be willing to be flexible and to look at the things that don't work well—in your company and in your style of leadership—with the same gusto and vigor that you bring to solving problems or dreaming up next-level innovation. *Find the issue and upgrade the shit out of it.*

Let's talk about hot chocolate for minute so that I can demonstrate this philosophy in action. Sometimes, you might have a boss who doesn't want feedback or won't entertain a proposed change because they're the one who made the decision in the first place and they're happy with it. This has happened *many* times in my career and it's important to understand that your resilience muscle will come into play here, too. So here are three words for you: Backwards Hot Chocolate.

When I was working at one particular food company in my early management years, a lot of the food and menu decisions were arbitrary. There were things like, "My wife thinks we should have hibiscus tea on the menu because she and her friends like it, and she says it's very trendy now—make it happen." You can imagine the eye rolls and groans I got from the food developers when I told them why we were looking at a product like this herbal tea as a menu addition—after they had already researched and thoughtfully made their beverage suggestions. Yet we had to bump them all for "the wife."

At some point, one executive decided to revamp the hot chocolate. I was so excited about this because hot chocolate, or *le chocolat chaud*, was an obsession of mine after living in Paris. The first time I had it in that city, I thought I had never in my life encountered such rich, velvety, creamy goodness all wrapped up in a thick, steaming hot, pourable beverage. I mean, let's call it what it is. *Melted chocolate that is drinkable!* There is nothing better in the world than *chocolat chaud* done properly. It is so sinfully good, you actually feel naughty when you're drinking it. Like, look-over-your-shoulder naughty.

Done properly, it is already made perfectly so there is no need to add anything like cream or milk. If you're ever on your way to the Louvre, just stop by Angelina on Rue de Rivoli right by the Jardin des Tuileries. *Chocolat chaud* is exquisitely made at Angelina. Or sometimes you'll find it served in cafés with a small pitcher of steamed milk or cream on the side so that you can thin it out if you want to. Sacrilege, in my opinion, but you do you.

This particular leader I mentioned before decided that he wanted hot pourable chocolate, and he put it on the menu with plain warm milk already... in the cup?! And a small pitcher of warm chocolate on the side? WTF. This concoction was *not chocolat chaud*. It was some watery beverage theater that tasted like normal, snooze-fest hot chocolate, not the rich, velvety European hot chocolate I knew. I was sure our customers would pay more for a proper *chocolat chaud* and not some watery Swiss Miss nonsense. It might not have been made from powder—true, it was a recipe that used good chocolate—but that actually stung even more because it could have been greatness and written about in every food section. But no, this leader did not want to hear about it. He was very happy with his version and did not see why it was *actually backwards*. It blew my mind. Younger-manager me lost actual sleep over this travesty. A lot of sleep.

It was super frustrating because he was not a chef and had no culinary degree; he had just his opinion and he was the boss. It didn't help that he would regularly boast about having a "super palate" and throw in obscure culinary words while eating like, "Umm... umami..."—a habit that did not exactly endear him to me or my team. *Pompous, much?* I persisted with trying to persuade him to change the recipe and explaining why—I mean, if you could create the best version of a product and introduce your customer to an experience that floored them while also ensuring profitability, why wouldn't you strive for that? It's ripe for the taking! *Come on!* But he just wouldn't hear about it. All I did was annoy the crap out of him, which did not set our relationship up well. And, while it was always "backwards hot chocolate" to me, the drink became a great success over time and was loved by customers. For years, I had to watch it get made multiple times a day and just let it go. Over and over again. That experience shaped my working relationship with that particular boss, and while I learned to bite my tongue and pick my battles, I'm sure that I damaged his perception of me by doggedly pursuing my own version of hot chocolate excellence over those months.

It can be painful to not be a decision-maker, but I am here to tell you that moments like this happen all the time—they did for me, and they will for you. You are not alone, and you can go scream into your pillow as often as you like. The muffled cries will be heard around the world by your fellow commiserates. In fact, my colleagues and I still giggle about the hot chocolate all these years later—remember what I said about the painful today becoming hilarious tomorrow? *So true.* In later career years, I discovered the joys of A/B testing, focus groups, and designated test locations so that personal opinions did not need to factor so hugely into large product decisions. But at that time, that's how the big decisions were often made. *I wasn't even allowed to test.*

From a career perspective, I would have been much better off keeping my own hot chocolate ideas on my Pocket List, accepting no as the final answer, and just letting it go until I had the authority to change the recipe down the road. *Easy-peasy.* From the perspective of the Management Big Five, while the business was thriving and customers were oblivious to any friction and loved their backwards beverage theater, I was on shaky ground: a leader was irritated, I felt like a culinary failure for allowing this travesty of a recipe on my watch, and my team was distracted. So maybe I earned, like, a C minus? My opportunity to learn here was significant on many fronts. Remember: *find the issue and upgrade the shit out of it.* The issue in this incident was me and my own hard-headedness—and upgrade I did.

So, commit here and now to take the hard lessons about yourself that you are going to discover in leadership and turn them all into grit as you maintain that resilience muscle and keep moving forward. Don't get in your own way, be willing to shake off the sticky ego traps that are holding you back, and be willing to let go of the old way of doing things. There is opportunity in everything—even in missed-opportunity hot chocolate—so learn to look for it. You're still in your "all that responsibility without authority" years. You'll have your time to do it your way soon.

Unleash Epic Momentum by Doing What Scares You

Embracing growth mode—embracing *vulnerability*—can also mean putting yourself into terrifying situations. It was certainly not my plan to out myself as a high school dropout to a few hundred managers, chefs, and business leaders who were in my org chart, but at one point in my leadership career that's exactly what happened. It was during a town hall meeting that was in-person and virtual, and I was presenting on a strategy that was continuously evolving due to some explosive growth we were experiencing. The pressure to keep up was on, and the entire organization was feeling the stress, as was I.

I read the "room" and felt that unmistakable "we'll never be able to achieve this" anxiety enter the space, and I decided in that moment to be totally authentic. I let the team know that I was *with* them, *for* them, and *one* of them, more so than they thought. I told the story of how I had overcome some pretty steep odds in my own career, and as I did so, I watched a new kind of energy take hold and push aside the sense of doubt that we would ever be able to achieve what we needed to. I think they were a little shocked to discover that their senior leader was a high school dropout, but it opened a new conversation that overwrote "how are we going to do this?" with "absolutely anything is, in fact, possible."

NOT Backwards Hot Chocolate, or *Le Chocolat Chaud* the Right Way *Dammit!*

ALL IN TAKES ABOUT 10 MINUTES • MAKES 2 SERVINGS

If you want to be all fancy about it, you can pour this hot chocolate into a jug and then pour into the mugs at your table in front of your guests. A little bit of theater is always good! And if you want to have even more fun (more fun than drinking pourable chocolate?!), you can flavor the whip with booze. OMG, so good.

8 ounces dark chocolate (70% Valrhona is best for this recipe, but any brand will do)
DO NOT use chocolate chips because the stabilizers won't make for a nice, finished product—really!

1½ cups whole milk

½ cup heavy cream

2 teaspoons granulated sugar

½ cup heavy cream, whipped
Always serve the whipped cream on the side because it melts so fast.

Set up a bain-marie (double boiler!) by placing a heatproof bowl over a pot of simmering water. Add the chocolate (preferably in rough chopped pieces) to the bowl and melt until it reaches a smooth consistency.

Meanwhile, in a separate pot, heat the milk, heavy cream, and sugar to just about a simmer—be careful not to let it boil. *Look for any bubbles forming on the sides and you will know to remove the pot from the heat.*

Add the melted chocolate to the warmed milk, cream, and sugar and whisk well until it reaches a smooth, creamy consistency. Pour directly into mugs and serve with the whipped cream on the side.

Honestly, between you and me, before this meeting I would have preferred to drop my pants and reveal a boil on my ass than let a thousand team members know that particular piece of information about me, but in that moment my fears were eclipsed by the realization that my own insecurities could become strengths for all of us if I was willing to take a leap. So I did.

It is worth noting that the reason I took that leap was that I myself had experienced leaders who had chosen the path of vulnerability in unexpected moments, and I had watched as it led us all into a position of unparalleled courage and strength. One genuinely life-altering moment in my career was when a cabinet member of California's government came up to me after a Los Angeles City Council hearing, where I had been called to publicly testify on the GMO debate on behalf of the Los Angeles Food Policy Council. As I made my case for more transparency in food labeling, an issue that is still deeply important to me, I shared with everyone who was tuning in—yes, these hearings were broadcast on live television—that I was a nervous public speaker. I think I also made a joke about needing to breathe into a "brown bag" or something ridiculous like that. Gah! *Always with the nerves!*

After the hearing, a leader sought me out, pulled me aside, and said, "My wife made me go to Toastmasters. It gave me a lot of confidence, because I hated public speaking, too! You're better than you think you are, so stick with it." I mean, he didn't even know me! That this leader took the time to find me and openly share his own journey so he could let me know that I was not alone—well, let's just say that even today I always silently thank him before I step up to do any major public speaking event, and he is always in my heart. What a world-class leader and human.

Another CEO, who oversees a billion-dollar global food company, broke down in tears in a senior leadership meeting when discussing a work incident that had cost the life of an employee. He shared with the two hundred or so folks in the room that he carried the employee's photo in his wallet to remind him every day of what was most important. Seeing their leader unexpectedly reveal his emotions in such a candid and solemn way over a horrendous incident that no one would ever want to happen on their watch made his team understand that the safety and care he was advocating for was not just to tick off a box. This was a deeply personal mission, rooted in both personal and corporate responsibility, and his vulnerability helped them truly see that they needed to make certain that their decisions for the business would protect human life now and in the future.

Two different leaders who were in the room told me that they would never forget this genuine moment of raw, tender leadership. It stays with them as a guide of sorts, showing them the way as they shape their strategies and execution plans for the tens of thousands of employees at that company.

As it turned out, my "hey, I'm a high school dropout" moment also had a lasting impact and led to some frank and impactful conversations about the need for leadership engagement and better communication at every level of the business. Information was not trickling down the way it needed to in order to support the folks at the entry level of the business. Some of this was because we needed to do a better job of relatable storytelling to inspire and motivate, but some of it was also because many employees and managers were afraid to share information in an "out loud" kind of way. For people at all levels, there was the sense that putting yourself out in the open—what you know, what you don't know—was unpleasant and uncomfortable, and many just didn't want to take the risk.

As I received this feedback, I realized that I could probably move the needle faster by getting personally involved with more direct connection and communication. I could help crack open team confidence by revealing more of myself. So, I started making time to show up at all sorts of meetings at every level of the business. In doing so, I learned firsthand about the obstacles and communication issues being experienced by junior managers and supervisors, issues that largely had their roots in a lack of self-confidence. By openly sharing my personal stories of mistakes I'd made—alongside the expectations I had for their performance—I think I helped many of these people get out of their own way. They needed to hear what I had needed to hear when I was climbing the ranks, and I needed to be open and vulnerable enough to give them that perspective in a truthful and relatable way.

We're all just winging it most of the time. All of us. People want to know that their leaders are just as imperfect and human as they are. If you can create an open, collaborative environment, you will be able to unleash epic energy, productivity, and innovation; you just have to be willing to go there. It's the ultimate way to foster active, ongoing bravery in your business. You can be both things at once: an incredible professional *and* an imperfect, mistake-making human. If you allow room for growth in yourself, you will open that same door for others as well, and the energy, buy-in, progress, and innovation you unleash will be *huge*. You'll see what I mean when you do. I promise.

TIME TO GET INTO MISE MODE

**Your prep for embracing the discomfort
and keeping yourself in growth mode.**

MINDSET SHIFT: When you understand that *everything* is a learning opportunity, then, magically, all those mistakes and mishaps will turn what can feel like shameful garbage into fertile nutrients that will build your managerial muscle.

TRADE SECRET: When you're feeling in over your head, remember this magic phrase: *We're all just winging it most of the time.* Your colleagues and even your bosses have been there, too, whether they admit it or not. Being open and offering your team the gift of your vulnerability will bring people together to find solutions in deep and powerful ways.

LEADERSHIP LOWDOWN: Nothing stays the same, and great leaders know they need to be constantly innovating and improving. And that doesn't just apply to your brand or business practices—it also applies to you and the way you do things. Be real with yourself and recognize that continuous career growth demands continuous improvement.

INSIDER DISH

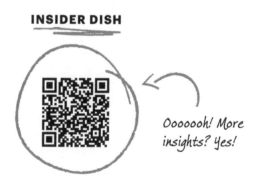

Ooooooh! More insights? Yes!

11

LET'S BREAK BREAD AND CHANGE THE WORLD

How *You* Can Create a Healthier, More Sustainable Industry

If not us, then who?

If not now, then when?

AS YOUR JOURNEY takes you further into leadership, you will reach a point in your career when money and job titles provide only so much satisfaction. That's when you'll understand that real satisfaction comes from the fuel underneath it all. *Your purpose.* All the daily work you engage in over the years, whether you know it yet or not, is adding up to your "reason for being." I've already told you about my personal career mission: executing fresh, responsibly and transparently sourced food that I would be proud to serve my grandmother. Beautiful, nutritious, *real* food at enormous volume. Millions and millions of meals. *Impact.* Over the course of my career, access, affordability, and job creation became my "reach" goals. I wanted to drive positive change for the industry by helping others find their way and challenging folks to stay the course and not let anyone or anything get in the way of their dreams. These aims became the treasured, heartening thread woven through it all.

So, with all that in mind, I want to ask you an important question: What is your personal career mission? How are you going to make your mark on the world once you reach a place where you can really move the needle? As poet Mary Oliver famously said, we only have one wild and precious life. What big things will you do?

I mean, what's it all for—the blood, sweat, tears, learnings, angst, failures, triumphs—if not to do all the things we are capable of?

That process of discovery starts now, at whatever point you're at in your career. Because by the time you reach executive leadership, you will be able to enact the change you want to see. Your job now is to uncover what you care about and what those changes look like. Step one in finding your purpose? Opening your eyes and truly grasping the knowledge that, whether you're a line cook in a diner, a social media manager for an energy bar company, or a determined food entrepreneur selling your homemade jams at the farmers market, you are part of a global industry that has the single most profound impact on the lives of every person on the planet. Did you know this about the food world and its crazy opportunity for deep, world-changing impact? *It's absolutely true.*

This is the real reason I love this industry: The taste of opportunity is not just about me and it's not just about you. It's about the whole damn world. The food world has the unparalleled capacity to lead the way in taking care of each other and the planet—making the world healthier and more equitable and habitable—and together, we need to do a much better job of harnessing that incredible opportunity. I mean, food is squarely at the center of some of the biggest issues of our time, and if you stay in this industry, make it your career home, and get to the top, you—yes, *you*—can make a meaty, life-altering, global impact on issues that are urgent and significant.

Massive Company = Massive Impact

Do you think that seventeen-year-old Ingvar Kamprad knew that he would become a world-renowned entrepreneur and globally impactful CEO of a business with $45 billion in annual revenues and a demonstrated commitment to sustainability? That's the founder of IKEA, by the way. Yep, the furniture company whose commitment to sustainability has been a trailblazer in showing the business world how to turn values into impactful practices in their everyday operations. Why am I talking about IKEA, of all things? Because IKEA also happens to be one of the ten largest food retailers in the world, selling—for just a start— over a billion meatballs each year. *So. Many. Meatballs.*

Long ago, Mr. Kamprad recognized that offering food to his customers would lead them to stay longer, so he started selling coffee and sandwiches in his early stores through the 1950s. Eventually, he expanded to house full restaurants in the stores. Today, IKEA has leveraged its massive influence to forward its values, committing to provide 50 percent plant-based restaurant meals, eliminate plastic packaging by 2025, and use only recycled and renewable materials by 2030. So, basically, a teenager with a passion for selling everyday items to everyday people went on to create the largest furniture business of all time *and* one of the largest food businesses in the world over the course of his life. In doing so, the company he built, his legacy, is leading the charge in demonstrating how businesses everywhere can live by example and still be wildly successful.

If you care about your personal impact on the world's ecosystem—environment, climate, people, animals, everything—and I believe you do—then you surely see the opportunity, too. Remember, real sustainability is about *sustaining and maintaining* our collective current impacts and ensuring that we are leaving things as we found them for the health of future generations. Hopefully, we are also improving things along the way.

Where does that start? With telling the truth.

There are such big issues to tackle in this industry: Massive, extraordinary, and, frankly, disgraceful waste at all levels; an often mysterious supply chain that is not always ethical and definitely not sustainable; and a lack of transparency and consumer awareness surrounding food additives, coupled with intentionally confusing laws supporting the insane mystery in the labeling and processing of our food that, in some cases, risks undermining the very foundation of what food is for: to sustain our health. *Yep, "natural flavor," I'm looking at you.* We have so much to do, and so much opportunity before us. Today is the perfect day to get cracking on this.

Because if not us, then who? If not now, then when?

Emma Watson said something very similar in her UN speech about gender equality. Though she was talking about a different issue, the sentiment is very relevant here: What's it all for if not to do all the big things that we are capable of?

"Nothing in Here but the Good Stuff"
Grilled Lamb Lollipops
With Lemon, of Course!

ALL IN TAKES ABOUT 40 MINUTES • ACTIVE TIME 35 MINUTES

SERVES 4 HUNGRY MEAT EATERS

I like to serve these on a big platter in the center of the table and just let everyone go to town. In the summer, I serve them with a big, gorgeous, fresh salad full of herbs and veggies, crusty artisanal breads like a baguette or sliced sourdough boule (and always with a nut, olive, or fruit bread, too), a selection of gorgeous hard and soft cheeses like Midnight Moon and a ripe Camembert, and good butter (Kerrygold in the gold wrapper always works!). All of that alongside a lovely, easy-to-drink, perfectly balanced pinot noir is the chef's kiss. (Donald Patz's Maritana Vineyards is my fave California producer of kick-ass pinots.) In the cooler months, these lamb lollipops are perfect with roasted garlic mash and roasted veggies. Honestly, they are perfect with everything, so you really can't go wrong.

You should prepare the chops in advance and store in the fridge until you are ready to grill and eat. But! They have to be grilled à la minute. Don't even think about grilling these in advance.

Have your butcher break down the lamb racks into individual chops if you aren't sure how to do it. Also, get fresh lard from the butcher while you are there. One-stop shopping always wins in my book.

---

3 lamb racks, cut into individual chops, bone in each chop

4 ounces fresh pork lard, melted in a saucepot

Maldon sea salt and freshly ground black pepper, to taste

2 lemons, cut into wedges
Reserve ½ a lemon for the final seasoning of the chops.

Start prepping the chops a few hours before you intend to serve. First, melt the fresh lard in a saucepot over the stovetop and hold aside. On a cutting board, pound and flatten each individual chop either with a mallet or by holding the back of a chef's knife flat against the round, meaty part of the chop (not the bone) and whacking the knife with your closed fist until the meat has flattened and expanded. *Obviously, hold the knife flat and don't cut yourself!* Hold in a pile on a plate until all the chops are flattened.

Prepare a large tray or plate lined with parchment and have several more parchment sheets at the ready so you can easily separate each layer of lard-covered meat before you wrap it in plastic. *As the lard sets over the chops, it can get quite messy, and the parchment will help keep everything in place until it's time for grilling.*

One by one, drag the pounded-out part of the chop into the melted lard—just enough to coat. Immediately place the lard-covered chop flat on the waiting lined plate or tray and sprinkle with Maldon on the top side. Repeat until you have 1 layer of chops, then add another parchment sheet so that the meat is essentially sandwiched between 2 layers of parchment.

Repeat this until all the chops are coated, seasoned, and lying flat on the parchment. Normally, I end up with about 3 layers of parchment and chops—about 6 chops on each layer—side by side (never touching), kind of like a parchment paper and raw-lamb-chop layer cake. Finish with a layer of parchment on top, wrap the whole thing with plastic wrap, and place it in the fridge. *It's important to do it this way because it makes it easy to grill and eat later on. Also, no mess!*

When it's time to eat, remember that these chops cook super fast, so don't get distracted. Fire up your grill to medium-high heat or have the charcoal grill hot and ready to go. With tongs, add the chops by the bone to the grill surface until an even layer is achieved. Season again with Maldon and grill for 1½ to 2 minutes per side for medium-rare. Remove and hold on a serving platter while you do the rest of the chops. *Sometimes I steal a chop or two as I'm grilling, to check for "doneness."*

Give a final sprinkling of Maldon (you want these well seasoned!) and grind some black pepper overtop. Squeeze half a lemon over the chops and serve with a pile of lemons on the side. Eat!

But first, a moment. When we need to talk about divisive and uncomfortable things, it always helps to start from a place of togetherness and generosity. So, let's picture ourselves sitting at a beautiful knotty wood table draped in a simple muslin cloth. We are outside; it's a breezy, late summer day and the sun has just disappeared over the mountains. The sky is all sorts of fire. The wine is flowing, Röyksopp's "Remind Me" is playing quietly on a speaker somewhere, and the table in front of us holds a generous supper of lovingly made dishes brought by each of us. The grilled lamb lollipops and the hint of lemon wafting off them smell extraordinary. Citrus and olive trees graciously watch over us, and we feel warm, happy, and comfortable as our bellies start to grumble. Our collective energy is full of stirring, gently aching anticipation as we await discovering more of "the possible." We are ambitious. We are hungry— *for food, for change.* "Pot-lucky" we are, indeed.

Why the Food You Serve (And Where It Comes From) Really Matters

Growing up, I saw firsthand the physical challenges that unhealthy food creates. My father was a diabetic, and he lost his life after a battle with kidney and heart problems. He had an insatiable hunger for fast, cheap food that I believe contributed to his early death at the age of fifty-two. I was twenty-three when this happened, and it was while I was at the brokerage, sourcing ingredients for some of biggest food manufacturers in America. As I learned more about the food industry through those early years of my career, I saw that while there were many brilliant and amazing things people were doing around food—especially in product development—the industry could also be destructive, abusive, and sneaky, creating harmful choices for people, and for the world. I was genuinely surprised and, frankly, disgusted.

All the stealthy ways in which some food companies, with their big budgets and market share, would intentionally manipulate our five senses through both product development and marketing outright shocked me. My head was constantly exploding: *Wait ... this is allowed? This is legal? You can put actual chemicals on the shelf and get away with not telling people what they are consuming? Because labeling laws protect the businesses and not the consumers? WTAF.*

While I was deeply disturbed by what I discovered, I was also so full of hope and promise for what *could* be done instead of what *was* being done. *There had to be a better way.* That's when I first made that promise to myself—to do things differently and "strive for better"; to learn how to put beautiful, fresh food out in the world—which led me to culinary school, which then only strengthened and solidified my personal food values.

I never would have guessed that living in Paris and seeing the daily experience of French food values would influence me so strongly as a professional: everyday farmers markets, bakeries that made and sold fresh, beautiful breads daily, artisanal cheese shops where butter was just as precious as a true Brie de Meaux, open-air fish markets . . . I mean, I learned more from my experience of living and eating in France than I actually learned from culinary school. Sure, Le Cordon Bleu gave me the tools and techniques I needed to bring the food experiences I treasured to life, but I couldn't possibly have known without having lived it what larger influence the experience would bring to my personal values. It was a true privilege, and I recognize that not many others will have this same kind of opportunity. But I hope that, as I share these experiences, you can recognize the places in your own life where you felt or learned something similar.

As my career progressed from culinary student to executive chef and on to food and beverage management, both the weight and meaning of my personal commitments evolved in surprising and unplanned ways. Working side by side with folks who were, and still are, commonly referred to as "illegal" or "undocumented" was deeply impactful. I couldn't understand why the simple fact that this critical part of the workforce pays actual taxes and contributes enormously to our shared economy was rarely, if ever, discussed.

I already knew this from having my own fake ID back in my teenage working years: there's no way around paying taxes when you have a job that generates payroll. You can't, like, just opt out. But, just for some context, in 2019, undocumented workers from Mexico alone contributed an estimated $9.8 billion in federal, state, and local taxes in America, and another almost $14 billion in social security and Medicare contributions. They also spent about $82.2 billion while contributing massively to local economies. Oh, and approximately 96 percent of undocumented Mexican workers are *on payroll*—one of the highest employment rates in the country. But sure: use "illegal" as a description for a hard-working, fully contributing member of society. *Not.*

As my career progressed, I became even more aware of the challenges of immigrant workers in our country. I was embarrassed and frankly enraged by the incomprehensible lack of respect for the largely immigrant farm workers who graciously withstood the toughest conditions you can possibly imagine to bring our food to the table all day, every day. I mean, seriously—imagine spending every working day in temperatures that can reach more than 100 degrees, bent over for hours on end, picking teeny berries off stems with your fingers so that someone else can have fruit on their granola every morning—and all for $8 an hour. I'm talking *heroes,* who deserve some damn respect and gratitude along with a decent living wage. And let's be clear—this work requires skill. To say "unskilled" when describing a superhuman ability to withstand and triumph in such conditions for years on end is flat-out wrong. *The people who do these jobs are an invaluable and highly skilled workforce.* And then there is the meat industry. And the trash industry... and... I think you see my point.

The significance of lived experience and all of the insight you will gain that will, in turn, impact your values and inform your unique purpose is massive. My commitment to fresh food ultimately evolved into a vision for executing massive, extraordinary volumes of fresh, nutritious, delicious, high-quality food at scale for the maximum possible impact. That purpose has guided me through all of my management roles and eventually into oversight of some of the world's most visible food and beverage programs. The organizations I chose to work for, and the food and beverage offerings I chose to put my time, reputation, thought, and energy into, mattered to me and were very intentional. Sure, I heard a lot of comments over the years from bosses and colleagues—"why do you care so much?" "what difference does it make?"—but I knew that, somehow and in some way, what I put out into the world could make a teeny, tiny difference. You may have that feeling, too, and I am here to tell you: *go with it.* It all absolutely matters, and it will be the fuel you need to get you through the challenging moments.

I know you see problems in this industry. *I see them, too.* I'm not here to tell you to ignore them and focus on your career instead; I am telling you to pay attention, and to start delving into these issues and how they affect your life, the people you care about, and the whole world. If you keep your eyes open and your intentions true, you will absolutely start to change the things you want to change.

So where do you want to focus your impact? If you care about human trafficking, then start looking at where you could have influence in supply chain work. If the crushing weight of the garbage that we humans generate concerns you most, then look at all those opportunities for change in issues like food waste, disposable "compostable" containers that have practically no hope of ever being composted (yes, pretty much everyone knows this, but no one wants to say it out loud), or recycling systems that don't actually recycle. (According to the US Environmental Protection Agency, only 10 percent of the plastic generated since recycling started in the 1960s has actually been recycled. Ten percent! *This whole time!*) There is so much meaningful work to do here—just Google "extended producer responsibility" and you'll see some starting points for accountability and solutions that we can all get excited about.

Care about where your food comes from, and how the people and lands that produce it are treated? Start looking for companies with transparent food principles, or perhaps an organization that is endeavoring to create a universal sustainability certification system. Even just pushing your current employer at each stage of your career to commit to more transparency is a way to have impact. *Small actions matter greatly.* Progress is progress, even when it feels like a tiny step.

Or maybe your priority is more about what exactly is *in* that food. I personally think that the USDA "dietary plate"—yes, the one that shows the "correct" balance of food groups in our diets—should include a small area for chemicals, just so we can begin to understand the health impacts of our daily excessive consumption of food additives that are currently not calculated or studied yet somehow supported by our government. *Wait, what?* Yes, it's true. Remember when I called out "natural flavor" at the start of this chapter? Now and for the past six decades, the FDA has inexplicably allowed food companies to hide synthetic chemicals as "natural flavors" under the guise of proprietary recipe protection or "trade secrets." You are consuming them whether you like it or not, so let's add it to the issues plate so we can actually talk about it, and—just maybe—you could even start doing something about it in your own career.

It's all a lot to take in, I know. But you need to know now that there is nothing that will get us to solutions faster than coming to understand how important and powerful your own contribution can be. So, make this moment your starting point, if you haven't begun already. And then start looking ahead to figure out where you could expand your impact in the years to come.

Change Is Always a Work in Progress

Let's return for a moment to our "changing the world" potluck picnic. If we were to collect our mise for this potluck, there's just one ingredient that would have the most impact on our ability to succeed at the planetary impact level, and that's compromise. Why? Because *imperfection is where the magic happens.*

Embracing imperfection—or compromising—is how we drive the relentless pursuit for improvement in ourselves, those around us, and our collective work. It's how we manage our personal standards, how we know when we want to change something and even wish for something different, more, or better. Imperfection is basically the greatest gift in our lives: it's the universal catalyst for change, and it reflects the constant state of both people and the world. *You know—"in progress."*

And if we are real with ourselves and acknowledge that we constantly make trade-offs in our professional lives, perhaps we can stop pointing at one another and just join forces for all of our sakes. For years, I have listened to sustainable food people I love and respect complain that "Big Corporate" is at the table at conference X, or on this panel at event Y.

To be honest, in my earlier days, I used to be one of those people—right up front: "Get outta here, you don't belong here, you folks created this mess and we're trying to clean it up." But now I can see how incredibly foolish and shortsighted that was.

We need "Big Corporate" at the table, and, frankly, the folks who have been brave enough to show up at these conferences deserve some mighty credit, because I'm sure they've often felt like they are being fed to the sharks. The hard truth is that we are stronger and better together, and we should be inviting Big Corporate to our table with open arms. Working together—solving together—dreaming together. Don't you see? We can accomplish extraordinary things when we are impacting millions of people instead of hundreds. We can leverage the power and strength of bigger organizations and work *alongside* them to change and improve things. It's smart, it's strategic, and, most importantly, it will create change *faster*.

Know what two factors really drive systemic change in the food world? *Demand from consumers, and the cash to make it happen.* That's pretty much it. No big company is going to change anything if their customers aren't asking for it (and willing to pay), and no company of any size can make changes without that demand and the cash. Big change costs big money, and, as I've said before, money doesn't just fall out of the sky.

So, we have to compromise. We all have to make trade-offs. *Fact.* We can make trade-offs and move the needle at the same time. *Also fact.* We don't need perfect solutions; we need traction, incremental progress, and shared goals. We need to use our individual roles in the food world to influence, educate, and push for the changes we want to see and care most about, as a junior floor manager, as a regional supervisor, at the head office, and, eventually, in the executive suite.

The TikTok Acceleration Factor

Here's another thing to consider: if we want to create awareness around certain topics and drive planetary change faster, we have to make everything *cool*.

Wait—what? Cool? What has that got to do with my values and future impact?

Well, as it turns out, a whole heck of a lot.

Back when I started to notice what was shifting in the world—specifically around the convergence of personal health and public policy, and the food world not integrating well with either area for the benefit of the consumer—a few life-changing things happened that solidified my personal mission around food and what I wanted to spend my time on. One of those pivotal experiences came in 2010, from an unexpected moment in a food systems design meeting at the Federal Reserve Building in downtown San Francisco.

Larry Keeley, a world-renowned innovation and design expert, was leading a working group discussion on "the process of change" and how long it actually takes to move societies through necessary but not-yet-desired shifts. The two examples he used—seat belts and cigarettes—were a fascinating case study in just how extraordinarily long it takes to change the minds and hearts of Americans... and particularly to change our behaviors.

Just think about it. While seat belts have been available in cars since the late 1960s, the policy wars and laws only started to come about in the 1980s. And people were pissed! They thought their personal rights were being violated, and that no one, especially the government, was going to tell them what they could and could not do. Today, seat belts just seem like common sense—simply click and go. But decades ago, this topic was just as divisive as the debate over face masks during the endless COVID-19 pandemic.

Similar battles took place over cigarettes and smoking restrictions. Each issue took years—decades!—to gain the kind of traction with the public that would move the needle forward on policies. As Keeley's team walked us through the change process, a tidal wave of realization washed over me. No wonder change is so damn hard for everyone—even when it's for our own benefit, it literally takes fifty years to turn an idea into a fully supported behavior in the public domain, one that comes with actual accountability.

Fifty years. Mind. Blown.

According to Keeley's team, with all of their collective PhDs, incredible research, and experience, there was one way to speed up this time frame: make whatever you want to change *cool*. *Cool!*

I can't even put into words how much this resonated with me, how inspired I was, and how I immediately felt compelled to achieve systemic change in the food world in much faster time than fifty damn years. I mean—who has time for that? *I'll be in my eighties.* Not nearly good enough.

Over the next decade, I watched as social media took the world by storm and allowed people to jump on viral initiatives to be a part of a *cool* conversation. Remember planking? Or the ALS ice bucket challenge? Even Oprah Winfrey, Tyler Perry, and Bill Gates were jumping at the opportunity to have a bucket of ice-cold water poured over their heads—in part to promote awareness for a terrible disease but also because, well, it was cool. This is where TikTok and all the other conversation-driving platforms come into play. There is so much new opportunity to ignite these much-needed conversations and bring fresh awareness to all the wild opportunity to create an impact. *Can someone start a dance-off for this, please?*

So, if we need to be swish or rad or [insert whatever slang folks are using now] to bypass decades of churn and inaction and finger-pointing in the food world, where does that compromise actually need to happen? Well, pretty much everywhere. And while I don't have the perfect answer to igniting public interest and launching rapid change, I have been in the position to glimpse the arena where the answers are going to be found. And I, for one, am really excited. I mean, I'm talking Lady-Gaga-jumping-off-the-roof-at-the-Super-Bowl, best-halftime-show-of-my-life excited, because I know that this arena is made up of the people who are reading this book right now—the ones who are just starting out, who see what needs to be done, and who aren't tied down by the old ways of doing things. *You. Glorious and deeply important YOU.*

But listen: This is the long haul. If you want to make change, don't let yourself get discouraged. I adore the old saying that goes: "There is only one way to eat an elephant: a bite at a time." Small bites are the progress we need in every moment. In fact, *those small bites are also you*. Staying purposefully driven to improve and do better should be a shared goal for all of us, foodies or not. Everyone deserves to eat beautiful, nutritious, delicious food—and to be able to find it, afford it, know what's in it, and responsibly dispose of it. *All of us.*

These problems are big and messy and dire, but they are ultimately solvable. And if you make the food world your career home and ultimately *stay* in this industry, I believe wholeheartedly that you will be an instrumental part of the solution. At every stage in your career, you will have the opportunity to nudge your bosses to care about these issues, to ask questions that ignite deep internal thinking and strategy, and, eventually, to push your organization to make incremental improvements for the sake of progress, transparency, and overall human and environmental health.

Wild, epic, world-changing opportunity is now in your hands.

So, what are you going to do?

TIME TO GET INTO MISE MODE

Your prep for changing the food industry for the better, both as a future leader and from where you are today.

MINDSET SHIFT: Incremental progress is made *bite by bite*, using our voices and influence until a better outcome is achieved. Don't underestimate the power of compromise and bringing more people to the table to share your goals.

TRADE SECRET: Most people don't think about food beyond their direct experience: it came from the shelf, it lives in the blue bin, and if it tastes like lime or mesquite or cheddar, that's probably what it is. As a food-industry professional, you are in a position to look deeper. Educate yourself about labeling laws, waste practices, labor policy reform, and producer responsibility (or anything else that creates churn inside of you), because real change starts with the truth.

LEADERSHIP LOWDOWN: It takes *years* to make people change their behaviors. *Decades.* Stay committed, think long term, and look ahead to the impacts you can make at each step on the ladder. And in those moments when you really want a shortcut? Remember to think *cool.*

INSIDER DISH

More incredible insights here— check it out!

12

FROM MANAGEMENT TO EXECUTIVE LEADERSHIP

Serious Impact Is at Your Fingertips

It's time to stop doing
and start leading.

IMAGINE THIS: You are now far from the role that brought you into the industry. Long gone are the days of standing behind the dish station, driving the forklift, or perching on a ladder taking inventory—those places where success is all about your ability to execute with your own two hands. Now, you work mostly at a desk, in a conference room, or perhaps even in your car if you are a multi-unit operations leader. Your daily working life is still all about food, but it's also all about people. Your success now depends on how you inspire and motivate others to perform and achieve your commonly shared goals.

As a junior manager, you will work side by side with your team. The people you lead will actually know you and your intentions and experience all of your many sides on a day-to-day basis. That makes it easier for them to support you when you make tough decisions and forgive you when you screw up. But when you get to the next level and beyond, the people who are affected by your decisions, and by your mistakes, will probably never have met you in person at all. *Huh?* That's right: if you don't handle things carefully, this is when you run the risk of becoming one of those faceless suits everyone complains about—the same ones you're probably complaining about right now.

This means the time has come for you to figure out how to be known by your team—how to pull them all together and win their respect so you can achieve strong team performance and results—when they don't actually know you. *Welcome to mid-level management.*

The silent transformation from management to leadership can be really hard to navigate, but this is another absolutely critical mindset shift. *It's time to stop doing and start leading.* Time to take all of that hearty, substantive grit and determination you developed at the earlier levels of your career—the same grit you are developing now, in your current roles—and rely on those qualities to keep you steady as you navigate and master this new world ahead. The strength and capacity of your resilience muscle will become a game changer at this point in your career, simply because the stakes are higher all the way around. The pressures you have felt at all the various stages of your career are all changing once again, and they are only getting more intense.

"Leader You" versus "Inner You"

The middle and senior levels of leadership are all about putting on your game face—you're not exactly "not you," you're just "leader you." It's about how you take direction from the top, especially when you don't agree with it, and turn it into everyone's shared success. *Spoiler alert: There will be more than a few moments when you don't agree with direction from the top. Can you still taste that bland backwards hot chocolate?*

Remember: Even at the most senior levels of leadership, everyone still has a boss, shareholders, and colleagues with company objectives that might conflict with their personal values or strategies for victory. Make no mistake about it: if you want to be successful in this phase of your career, you will need to rely on your ability to work well with others and motivate those around you *despite* your feelings when your ideas are not aligned and *despite* the fact that many folks in your organization may not know you personally. You are now responsible for business decisions that impact hundreds or even thousands of people, the vast majority of whom don't know you at all. Your ability to apply effective systems, tools, and next-level communications strategies is now your "make or break" quality.

Of course, you will experience some supremely awkward and exasperating situations. The good news is that every one of them has the capacity to fortify your ability to lead if you are willing to walk through the fire and take your learnings from the heat. I remember noticing this silent leadership mindset shift in action when my first corporate boss suggested (read: required) that I grab a flashlight and get on my hands and knees during field restaurant visits to look under refrigerators and other equipment for signs of dirt, pests, and other issues. It was literally one of the most challenging requests that I ever had because it instantly made me an asshole to the teams I was inspecting.

At first, some of them would get sassy and pretty darn angry about it. My inside voice completely agreed with them, and it felt totally over the top to do what I was required to do. *Don't mind me! I'm just on my belly under your large equipment looking for dead bugs and rodent poo. Having the time of my life—really! FFS.* Still, I was surprised by the level of vitriol some folks had in reaction to having their kitchens pulled apart, but as painful as it was for all of us, my boss was totally right: If I wasn't looking, who would? But can you just imagine someone coming into your place of business with the sole purpose of looking for problems? (Um . . . er . . . I mean opportunities?) Talk about a setup for being disliked. Further imagine trying to implement new processes and solutions to the issues you found with a team that has not exactly "bought in" (to say the least), and then leaving for another location the next day, not to return for perhaps a month or longer. Would the team on the ground even implement the changes? How could you show them you are on their side so you can all work together and make awesome things happen?

Ultimately, I found success by being up front on arrival and warming the teams up to what was about to happen. Depending on the level of "suspicion with a sprinkle of hostility" encountered, I took extra time to share stories and outcomes from other visits, and leaned on humor as my primary tool for gaining support. Once I realized that my management responsibilities had shifted—now, my priority was to earn buy-in from a team that did not know me—the whole "crawling around on my belly and pointing out issues" became secondary. Both pieces had to be in place to ensure our mutual success.

These experiences started to form a pattern I slowly began to recognize. The more effectively I communicated, and the more relatable that communication was, the more buy-in I got. That knowledge was deeply effective in paving my way from junior to senior management—

especially when I (as "leader me") was tasked with executing what seemed like implausible requests, where direction from the top made absolutely zero sense and I had to basically defend the indefensible.

Yep—I had to do this for years at one organization. I mean, just imagine working at a bakery with a core offering of fresh, gorgeous, artisanal bread and viennoiseries like freshly baked croissants and pain au chocolat and having to say, "Nope, we don't toast" to every single customer who wanted their bread toasted or croissant heated. *Not joking.* Some exasperated employees even started calling that business "The House of No" to describe how it felt to have to hold that line against some very irritated customers. "What do you mean I can't get my side of baguette toasted? There is an oven right there—just go put it in and toast it!" "Why can't you warm up my croissant? You have the equipment, don't you?" "You're a damn bakery—you don't toast bread? What the hell do you do, then?"

As we all know, American food culture dictates that people be allowed to customize and personalize pretty much anything and everything their hearts desire. Dressing on the side, no nuts, an extra hard-boiled egg instead of bacon, extra bacon instead of tomato, hold the cheese, add more pickles, burger medium-well hold bun, burger well-done extra cheese. You know the deal. We're all guilty of having these expectations around our meal orders, and we feel extremely righteous in our quest to satisfy our personal taste buds. So, I bet you can guess how well that no-toasting rule was received. *Not great.* But the founder, who had unyielding principles about certain ways of serving food, remained staunch about it. All the breads were super-high quality and freshly baked in the wee hours every morning. Some, especially the baguettes, were also baked fresh during the day. But what did that have to do with toasting it? Can't bread be fresh *and* toasted? Was this the right hill to die on? I mean, who doesn't love some old-fashioned toast? My mouth literally waters just thinking about a perfectly toasted fat slice of sourdough slathered in homemade pesto mayo with exquisitely ripe, chunky slices of Brandywine tomatoes piled on top with whatever in-season crunchy heirloom lettuce is available and finished with broiled strips of cherrywood smoked bacon that are flawlessly crispy while simultaneously meaty enough to add a substantial bite to the sandwich. *OMG. Just give me some toast now, and let's move on.*

But for at least a few years, toasting was not allowed. The founder believed toasting was only for bread that was old or of poor quality. *His* bread—this amazing, special, handcrafted bread—was neither old nor of poor quality. So. No. Toasting. Period. *The founder said so.*

Now, I was the person responsible for enforcing the food standards within this business, and I had to hold everyone accountable to those standards. Did I agree with this rule? *Nope. Not by a mile.* It made no sense to me to anger customers by not giving them what they wanted instead of making the sale, delighting them with nice, toasty whatever, and then just moving on. But my job was to enforce the policy, no exceptions, so I enforced it. Having the "why" allowed me to defend the rule and help the employees understand it. Even if I personally thought it was insane.

I share this piece of toasty weirdness with you because it's an example of the silent shift you will need to make between your near-future middle management behavior and your further-future leadership behavior, especially when you don't agree with direction from the top. As a manager, you might stomp around your restaurant and bitch and moan alongside your team about a ludicrous rule, and you might even let your servers go ahead and break it when no one from corporate is looking. But as a leader, you will have to find a way to move past your personal feelings, get your game face on, and inspire others to buy in to those decisions, to help them understand why they are made and hopefully come to respect them. *That's the silent shift in action.* In the Case of the DNT (Do Not Toast), while I didn't agree with that founder's position, I did respect the hell out of him as a leader and his unyielding food principles. He wanted it the way he wanted it. *So that was that.* It was my job to make it happen and get others behind the decision. The joys of leadership!

"Toasted Bread for Those Who Ask Should Be an Automatic YES" Ultimate BLT *Signed every person on the planet, FFS!*

ALL IN TAKES ABOUT 35 MINUTES • ACTIVE TIME 30 MINUTES

MAKES 2 COMPLETELY PERFECT SANDWICHES

Here's a pork lover's shout-out to the infamous Zingerman's Deli "Bacon of the Month Club"—something anyone interested in a deep dive into the world of bacon needs to check out. (Monthly smoky surprise in the mail, anyone? Sign me up!) The veggies are important, too, so if you have a green thumb and a yard or a big enough window box, I recommend ordering the Heirloom Seed Collections from Seed Savers Exchange and growing your own lettuce and tomatoes. I do this every year and it fills me with delicious joy.

1 package cooked (and still warm) bacon *It all starts and ends with the perfect bacon. Do not mess around with this. Nueske's triple-thick butcher cut applewood smoked bacon is a great place to start.*

1 loaf artisanal sourdough, sliced medium thick

1 batch "Leadership Lecithin" Mayonnaise (page 146) *Add fresh pesto to the mayo for an exquisite alternate version!*

2 handfuls fresh, tender summer lettuce leaves *Your pick, but the lettuce should be tender and a variety of colors if you can.*

4 large summer-harvest heirloom tomatoes, sliced thick

Maldon sea salt and freshly ground black pepper

2 glugs extra-virgin olive oil

Optional: ripe avocado slices, spread over the top

4 small bamboo skewers

Get all your ingredients together and ready to go. *The bacon should be made second-to-last. Toast the bread last, always, just before you assemble and only when you are ready to eat. If you toast the bread in advance, I'm afraid we can't be friends. "Sorry not sorry" situation.*

Grill your bacon over medium-high heat for 3 minutes on each side until golden brown or place the slices in a 400°F oven for at least 15 minutes. Hold the cooked bacon on a paper towel–lined plate to drain excess grease.

Slice 2 pieces of bread per sandwich and toast until crisp but still a tad chewy. *On a scale from 1 to 10, with 10 being burnt to a crisp, this should be a 7-8.* Spread a generous amount of mayo directly on the 2 bottom pieces and top with an evenly spread pile of lettuce.

Evenly spread out the tomato slices on top of the lettuce. Season the tomatoes with a pinch of Maldon, grind some black pepper over top, and then pour a little EVOO across the sandwich lengthwise.

Add the bacon slices evenly over the tomatoes. Cut them in half if you need to—it's totally fine.

Generously spread mayo over the 2 top pieces of toast and lightly press down over the bacon to close the sandwiches. Pop 2 bamboo skewers into each sandwich to hold everything in place while you slice down the middle on a diagonal, creating the ultimate BLT. Eat while it's warm!

Alert! Do not—I repeat, do not—refrigerate your tomatoes or even prep them in advance and hold them in the fridge. It dulls the flavor and destroys the texture. Keep 'em on the counter, folks.

Cross-Functional, Next-Level Aioli Time

"Leader you" versus "inner you" is also going to be critical to your success at this stage as you work cross-functionally with colleagues for perhaps the first time. This is a fancy way of saying that different areas of a business must work together toward achieving common goals. Think about your favorite soda from the market. So many different teams had to work together to get that drink on the shelf: marketing, logistics and distribution, product development, finance, procurement, legal, operations, and so on. As you continue to climb your career ladder, you will begin to work directly with other areas of the business to achieve your shared objectives. This means that you will gain more visibility across your organization and start to become known by more senior leaders. *Hello, my old friend "leadership lecithin"—what a pleasure to see you here!*

In the corporate food world, innovation and rapidly changing priorities mean that there is a constant push-pull dynamic between different areas of expertise: teams like operations, safety, marketing, facilities, and even R&D have to work together to solve all sorts of business challenges. (Good friction, remember?) Areas like procurement can often rub up against sales or operations because they have completely different goals, and while both are mutually important, sales and/or operations commonly get more resourcing and budget allocation because success or failure in those areas means measurable, obvious overall success or failure—instantly.

If you don't have sales, you don't have anything.

Procurement can be treated like a necessary but background function. Think about when you order your favorite pork carnitas. I mean, we all know that carnitas are the star of the show, but eating them without rice and beans? Or worse yet, without some fresh corn tortillas? *Sacrilege!* When looking at the significance of procurement in a business, ask yourself a simple question: If you don't "buy right," how in the heck are you supposed to maximize your profit potential? *Ooooooh, we get to talk numbers again! Yaaas!*

Set pure sales aside for a moment. A profitability ratio called EBITDA (earnings before interest, taxes, depreciation, and amortization) is the metric that most businesses focus on to understand what lies beneath a company's sales performance. If you earn $100 and your costs generated to make that $100 are $85 (including things like labor and goods), then $15 is your profit, right? But if your procurement team can negotiate better pricing, maybe those costs are now only $75 . . . so, your profit becomes $25. *See what I mean?* Same $100 in sales, a whole different level of profitability. EBITDA. Purchasing strategically might not be the "stunningly beautiful Zendaya" of the business in terms of headlining your movie, but its impact can be the difference between long-term success and failure no matter how many sales you generate. Procurement is basically Meryl Streep.

In practical terms, this can create friction across a business. Chefs might get annoyed that they are being "forced" to buy a particular brand of olive oil or poultry. On the business floor, you might hear, "Why can't I have an iPhone instead of this Android" or "Why can't I fly Southwest instead of American?" These decisions are all made with *purpose* if your leadership is maximizing their opportunities for profit. Whether that is communicated well or not is the question.

In fact, if any decisions like this are rubbing you the wrong way in your current role, ask yourself a deeper question: Why was this decision made? As a businessperson—*yes, you are now a business person*—you should want the company to make good choices around financial management so the business stays healthy and has a long runway ahead, even if that means you have to use a different brand of technology than you prefer. So yes, finger-pointing and tension between sales and procurement can be endless. But who is right? *Both and neither.* What's best for the business is right. Once you understand the underlying purpose, it becomes easy to say, "Just do your part to support and protect the business." (Bread and butter, baby—remember?) When faced with conflict or doubt, lean hard on that business tap to reach collaborative, mutual success. *Thanks, Management Big Five!*

Need more examples? Real estate and operations can also lead to conflict if they are not collaborating well with solutions in mind. The folks who manage real estate can find locations with incredible values and perks and can keep costs down with construction and design decisions, adding significantly to the overall bottom line. But often those decisions create operational quagmires. Maybe now a manager has to figure out how to get hot food to the dining room because the kitchen is on the other side of a long, busy hallway that cuts through a crowded mall. *Wait, what?* Yep, it happens, and worse, too. But the operations team can't exactly say, "Screw this, you guys deal with it." You have to make it work. That's the job.

This is what I mean about next-level, cross-functional aioli time. *A simple mayo won't do, anymore.* Middle-manager-you needs to level-up in order to deliver the dish and hit the spot with your customers. And make no mistake about it: your customers are now your colleagues. That's right, it's a whole new world again.

Listening to Interpret: The Brown Butter Technique

Let's talk tools for a moment. Processes, systems, and communication are your BFFs when it comes to leadership. Having your ear to the ground, reading the room, and knowing where to focus your energy are all ancillary components that will ultimately set you apart from your colleagues. Your ability to troubleshoot and problem-solve has now become a main part of your job function. So, of course, we need to talk about butter for a moment.

At some point, every aspiring chef has to master the skill of browning butter. Whether you are making sauces or baking cakes, simple "brown butter"—the nuttier, richer, instantly recognizable sister of regular ol' melted butter—is going to add that layer of depth you need to turn good into incredible. Making it is fairly basic—you melt unsalted butter in a saucepan or pot until it turns golden brown in color—but you have to take care because there is a really fine line between browning butter and burning it. The art lies in using your ears, not just your eyes, to determine when it's ready to remove from the heat. As the bubbling dies down, the crackling pops will start to soften and the tone will change, signaling that it is perfectly browned and ready to use. It's a very subtle shift, but it's impossible to miss if you *listen to interpret*.

If you're not listening to the crackling in this attentive way, you will miss that window and your butter will go from scrumptious and nutty to straight-up burned. *Yuck.* That's why browning butter is the perfect analogy for optimal people problem-solving. "Listening to interpret" is a necessary and fundamental skill for all effective managers. If you listen in the right way, you hear not only the words of the speaker but also the layers that exist *underneath* those words—layers that will be missed by those who only listen to respond. Using the Brown Butter Technique to tune into these layers of intent, mood, reaction—even true meaning—will supercharge your ability to work well with others, to problem-solve, and to negotiate solutions with effectiveness. It takes a special kind of leader to understand what is actually behind spoken words in complex situations, and being able to do so will set you apart from your peers at every level.

When I was a mid-level leader, I remember a very talented kitchen manager who had a difficult time dealing with stress. She would work so hard and was deeply involved in everything that came out of the kitchen, from early-morning prep to the busy service times. But her employees were complaining that she was mean and unpleasant, constantly yelling at them, and creating a hostile work environment. From their view, all she did was shout and tell them what they were doing wrong, and they were fed up with it.

When I sat down with this manager to understand what was happening from her perspective, she told me that her team was not working hard enough, that they weren't able to keep up with the rigorous pace that was needed, and that she was always ending up doing everything herself. She was overwhelmed, frustrated, and fed up, too.

On the surface, it seemed as if perhaps she was dealing with some incompetent or loafing staff, and she, the hero boss, was having to step in and make it all happen. *Of course* she was angry and exhausted! But by that point in my management career, I had learned the Brown Butter Technique of "listening to interpret"—so I was hearing what was lying underneath the words. What I also heard was that she was not taking the time to develop and train her team so that they could be more capable partners in the kitchen, and that she never allowed the pace to slow down enough to teach anyone. If someone didn't know how to do something, or how to do it quickly, she would push them aside and do it herself.

I mean, think about it: How is anyone supposed to be able to do something if no one shows them how to do it? Simple truths like this often get lost in the hustle and bustle of the day-to-day—it happens all the time. In this case, there were plenty of hands on deck; they just weren't empowered or trained to be effective. A failure of leadership? Yep. And easily solvable. She needed to take off her controlling hat, put on her coaching hat, and realize that the more she empowered her team with the knowledge and skills they needed to do their jobs, the better they would perform. *Ta-da:* less team stress, more teamwork enjoyment, and a leader who is free to focus on her management priorities.

As you first start to move into executive leadership and the demands on your attention come from more senior levels of oversight, you might be resistant to the idea of devoting your time and attention to deep listening, which admittedly can be incredibly frustrating. I can't tell you how many times I've had to sit and listen to immature, petty, and even ludicrous complaints from team members over the years. But honestly, in retrospect, I have been just as guilty of totally "cringetown" frustrations and complaints to my own bosses along my career journey. Frankly, everyone is. That's the thing! Even if something seems stupid to you, it likely matters to that employee in a real and serious way, and it will impact their performance.

When I look back at my own cringey rants, it was the leaders who took my feelings seriously—who took the time to listen, counsel, and add fresh perspective—who were the most impactful. And for the business, it was better for everyone. Energy was refocused, valuable learnings were gained through personal coaching, and a culture of respect was reinforced. Think of it this way: Aren't you more likely to work your ass off for someone who takes the time to listen to your challenges and help you through them? *I thought so.*

Before you say something like, "I couldn't do this if I had a team of a thousand people in my org chart," hear this: you could, and you will. *You have to.* Your teams are the ones who are executing whatever it is your business is trying to do, so any time and connection you invest in understanding what is really happening and how you should be applying resources will come back to reward you in extraordinary ways. *Really.* The folks who walk through fire every day—especially those on the front lines—have incredibly valuable insight, and you can learn a lot from them just by listening. That knowledge will impact your decisions, which will also help you to be known. So: The Brown Butter Technique. Use it.

There's One More Person Who Needs Your Leadership: *You*

Let's shift our attention back to that fifth pillar of the Management Big Five: *You.*

Now that you have a much greater understanding of the enormity of what's possible in this industry, along with some valuable tools and mise en place skills, it's time for me to ask you something deeply important.

What do you—yes *YOU*—want to achieve in this lifetime?

How do you want to make your mark?

I sincerely know that you will be able to accomplish whatever you set your mind to—that's the gift of the food world. Everything is possible and achievable. You just have to want it badly enough to tolerate the muck you'll have to wade through. So, let's talk about why resilience matters again, and why your commitment to your own career journey is the most important ingredient when you're working in Mise Mode. You, and only you, are the difference between achieving your dreams or not.

I had so many career moments when I just wanted to go home, snuggle with my cat, and pull the covers over my head and cry. In fact, I did exactly that more than a few times. My cat, Charlotte, became my honorary Personal Board Chairperson because of her amazing listening skills and unwavering loyalty. I vividly remember one particular career chapter, when it was proposed that I live in the apartment above one of the restaurants I was supporting. I immediately rejected this notion. I knew that the work would be incredibly demanding and I would need a place of rest, not a place where employees would be coming up to knock on my door at all hours of the day and night. I negotiated a different option, but once I arrived, the huge motivation and energy I was carrying for this project turned into confusion and anger when I realized that the living conditions they had set up for me were not only above one of the restaurants but also literally inside the actual office.

My "home" was a room next to the finance office, with a queen-sized bed and small TV in the corner. There were a shower and sink off to the side of the bed, but no toilet, and seemingly no door to the bathroom-minus-toilet setup. I was expected to use the office bathroom that was shared with the restaurant operators, receptionist, finance, and food teams. Can you imagine? Was I supposed to come out of the shower with my hair wrapped in a towel and greet my colleagues while I made my way to the bathroom? *What the actual fuck?*

I was so offended that the terms of our contract had been ignored that I called my old boss in outrage. He immediately offered to pay for a hotel room out of his operating budget while they figured out a solution. But the director who originally set up the project actually argued with me over the next several days and didn't want to pay for a separate place for me to live. It scarred our working relationship and he lost so much of my respect for not keeping his agreement (and for trying to make me feel like the asshole for objecting to an absurd and unprofessional situation). I never fully trusted him again. Thankfully, my PBOD assured me that I was correct to feel the way I did, and that I had the right to demand an appropriate, private, and safe space to live while I worked on this project—which I eventually got. There were exactly 126 stairs to reach the apartment they arranged for me, but I didn't care about that. I just wanted to be respected as a professional adult and provided a reasonable space to rest in my scant off-duty time.

I am sharing this story with you for a few reasons. Unexpected and ridiculous things are going to happen many times over the course of your career. *You* are a pillar on the Management Big Five for a reason—you can either let challenging experiences knock you off your game or you can decide to stay in it. I know, and I've said it many times already: staying in it can be way harder than quitting. But staying also means you will have the opportunity to write the rules differently one day—and that matters a lot.

As for this over-the-top, inappropriate situation? Well, it gave me the information I needed to understand that my values were not aligned with this company. I was a professional, but this leader showed me they did not really value or respect me. So, I quietly started looking for my next role in a place with more values alignment, and, in the meantime, I stayed and got the job done. I even got promoted, which ended up unlocking all sorts of opportunities I never could have anticipated. None of it was easy, but by keeping my dreams front and center and being curious about those burning questions—What do I want to achieve in this lifetime? How do I want to make my mark?—I found the fuel I needed to keep going.

Your Highest Calling as a Leader: Lifting Others Up

As you seek out respect for yourself, also remember that respect goes both ways. That brings us to the final mindset you will need to embrace as you head toward leadership. It's actually my most favorite thing about earning your way to authority. Here it is: The key to advancing to the highest levels in the food industry is not to *climb over* those above you, but to *lift up* those below you. Find the talent where it is hiding, build the skills where they are lacking, and then get out of the way to enable wild success for all involved.

In fact, raising others up and letting them shine is one of the greatest signs of an exceptional leader. I often think of an incredibly gifted chef who was tasked with overseeing part of the menu for a high-level executive innovation summit when he worked on my team. He was so ridiculously talented that he could easily have designed the whole thing himself and simply handed it to his team to execute. Instead, he turned toward his employees and asked them to explore their own personal culinary passions to come up with out-of-the box thinking on what this menu could look like. There was one entry-level cook on his team who loved creating herbal infusions, and she came up with the idea of unique all-natural popsicles that used ingredients with differ-ent nutritional and healing benefits—think artisanal apothecary meets culinary genius. They absolutely stole the show. Totally delicious, stun-ning to look at, rich in holistic value. They were basically the perfect embodiment of the innovative design that was the focus of the summit. Everyone talked about those popsicles for weeks and beyond, and all because this chef put his own abilities on the back burner and empow-ered his team to come up with something extraordinary. And, of course, he made sure that everyone involved knew that this success was *her* success, and that she got all the credit she deserved. Strong, confident leaders know that giving an employee the win does not take away from their own win. It amplifies it. And the business wins, too! *Bread and buttah, baby.*

Pay attention and you will see this dynamic at play on the highest stages in the food industry—and you'll see the opposite dynamic at play, too. Sometimes in the same place! Momofuku experienced wild success with the incredible creations of pastry chef extraordinaire Christina Tosi, inventor of such deliciousness as Milk Bar Pie and Cereal Milk. Chef David Chang obviously recognized her talent, gave her the oppor-tunity to create her own desserts, and then even encouraged her to open her own place—Milk Bar—when a space opened up next door to one of his operations. Today, Chef Tosi has opened a bunch of Milk Bar locations across North America and is living her entrepreneurial dreams, building what *Bon Appétit* called "one of the most exciting bak-eries in the country." *So freakin' cool.* But while Chang lifted Tosi up, he was also engaging in some pretty disturbing behaviors that have been widely reported, even by him, that served to alienate other employees under his watch and make them feel unwelcome in this industry. The result of Chang's apparent belief that you do not need to treat all people with respect and dignity in this industry has epically undermined what could have been a shining legacy. Such an incredible shame. Please, please don't make that same mistake with your own legacy.

Thankfully, there are more than a few voices calling for a more meaningful way of framing leadership. In 2010, I was attending a vision-ing workshop for a regional food systems project, and Stewart Brand, founder of the *Whole Earth Catalogue*, came in to give a talk. Brand is known for writing the book that anticipated the Internet and for his iconic tech visioning that was way ahead of its time. He was one of Steve Jobs's main influencers and is worth a Google search if you aren't familiar with his work. He said something to us like, "You have to remember that you aren't more valuable than someone else in your organization; you just have a different assignment."

To hear that kind of humble, plainly spoken view of checking your own importance while deeply valuing the contributions of others was extremely meaningful to me. *You are not better than anyone else just because of your role. You just have different responsibilities.* At every level of your leadership—from your first job as a shift supervisor to someday leading an entire company—you can actively choose to drive the performance of your team by lifting them up and letting them shine. Not only will you truly make a difference in the career paths of others, but you will also have an impact on the performance of the entire organization. And that will move you forward on your own career path. Besides, *it's just so awesome* to swing doors wide open for others and unlock their potential. Truly one of the best parts of the job.

All the Wrong Moves Are the Right Move

Wherever you are on your career journey and whether or not you know what's next for you, please keep this simple truth in your pocket: There is no such thing as a wrong move. You will learn and benefit from all of it. Especially the things that don't go perfectly or feel hard and unnecessarily painful.

The education of disappointment, or even of failure, is one of the unexpected things I have learned to cherish over my years. Even as the once-in-a-lifetime pandemic devastated massive portions of the industry I love, I watched as we came together in that adversity and learned lessons about resilience, compromise, and the profound, immeasurable value of our workforce. There are so many places in my own life's journey where I experienced pivotal, valuable moments of true growth, humility, expansion, and ultimately deep creativity and productivity because of disappointment and failure. We all need challenges to help us discover ourselves in deeper, more meaningful ways, and especially to learn what we value and hold dear.

Let me put it this way: With every new management role I've had, each one coming with new personal and professional challenges I could never have anticipated, I've learned something I didn't expect and that I have profited from. If I had to do it all over again, there is no role I would have skipped, no challenging leader or jackass colleague. In fact, I want to thank them all for the rich learnings they have provided over the years. All I have is gratitude and a full, thankful heart.

Perhaps now you can see why I can't stand it when I hear people talking about "dead-end jobs" in the food world, or people who focus only on all the things that are wrong with it. That's not the whole story, or even the real story. My whole career is a testament to "the possible," and yours can be, too. You just have to *stay in it* and hold your own dreams as paramount above everything else. It starts with that first promotion to shift lead—or warehouse supervisor or assistant manager or head hostess—and then it leads you to the next step, and the next. Eventually, you will get to a place where you can administer the experiences you want to share with the world and put your own values into action. There is simply no dream that is too small here. It's *all yours* for the taking. I can't wait for you to discover it all for yourself.

TIME TO GET INTO MISE MODE

**Your prep for nurturing and supporting the
future food-world leader living inside you.**

MINDSET SHIFT: There's "you," and then there's "leader you." When a decision comes down the line that doesn't seem to make any sense, "you" may think you know better, but once you reach mid-level management, you have to take a second to think again. Tap into "leader you" for the patience and insight to know when and how to enforce the decisions you don't agree with.

TRADE SECRET: When people are complaining, there is always more you need to hear than just their words. *Listen to interpret* by using the Brown Butter Technique to reveal the true issues at play.

LEADERSHIP LOWDOWN: The greatest leaders of the world know that real, spectacular, game-changing success doesn't come from inside their own heads; it comes from their *teams*. Helping unlock the genius and potential that lies inside the people around you is not just the secret to great results or your success—it's also one of the greatest joys of leadership.

INSIDER DISH

You don't want to miss these insights!

CONCLUSION
TASTE THE OPPORTUNITY

THESE DAYS, mornings are the most precious moments of my life. Well... so far, anyway. I am now in a season of rediscovering food through the lens of my beloved young daughter as she wakes up every morning to the wonder that is food. In her two-year-old mind, anything edible is super fun and even magical—especially when ice cream is involved. As she slowly emerges from her bedroom, she pulls my hand and leads me to the back door.

Waaas-bew-eee. Finga. Peeeeeez.

The raspberry bush is finally awake after a long, cold winter, and we are on "fruit watch."

We put on our garden shoes and venture outside and say good morning to "Heinz," the tiny vintage ceramic garden gnome with his luscious and overflowing basket of apples who keeps watch over the terrace. Then, we make our way around the herb garden, which is basically a mishmash of terra-cotta pots overflowing with everything from lavender to rosemary, lemon thyme, and sage. That's where we stop and say good morning to the "Emilie olive tree" that lives just next to the raspberry bush. *I love this tree.* I planted it when Emilie died; it watches over all of us and reminds me of the significant role my grandmother played in my life, and how that will, in turn, shape and influence my daughter. *Generational impact. Good morning, Emilie-loo.*

My daughter, Frankie, inspects for berries, plucks the dewy fruit and places each berry on a fingertip, then pops them into her mouth, one by one, finger by finger, the way we learned from the charming French movie *Amélie*. She moves Heinz from tree to tree until he is placed just so, and then we return to the house for breakfast making and baking. I roll out our weekly batch of sturdy, toddler-friendly sugar cookie dough so that she can make what can only be described as deformed yet delicious animal-shaped mini-cookies, predictably dumping way too much cardamom sugar on top.

Most days, we head out to the local farmers market, which fortuitously lives just outside of our apartment building. Farmer Paul sneaks treats to my girl, like shaved carrots that he knifes by hand when we approach, or tiny Topaz sour apples that he slips into her stroller. Just around the corner is the old-world bakery that makes everything on-site from scratch with its original recipes from the 1930s. We've gone there for fresh pretzel bread since her teething days, although now she prefers their tiny ham-and-pickle sandwiches and silver dollar-sized apricot jam cookies.

The joy in food that Frankie has already discovered makes my heart sing. I know that her play with flavor, color, and texture in these early years will have a quiet impact on the woman she becomes. As her curiosity deepens and her little fingers that push and pull the cookie dough become more skilled, her passion may very well be ignited. Will she be inspired to make the food world her career home or will something else bloom in her belly? *Time will tell.* As a parent, I wish that she will be brave enough to embrace what captivates and inspires her and to use "not knowing" as a sign of opportunity to discover what she enjoys, and doesn't, in order to guide her decisions about where to make her life's work.

I think the most valuable personal lesson I have learned over all these years is that you have to be willing to reach for the things you want for yourself. To simply try has probably become the most significant aspirational goal of my life, because when you do, wherever that attempt ultimately leads, not only can you win valuable learnings, but you can also take comfort in knowing that you were courageous enough to give it a whirl and see.

No regrets.

It's why I named my consulting company Essayer. It means "try" in French. I hope my daughter will find value in living by this philosophy so she never has to face regrets over things not tried in her life.

Truth be told, when I started my business, I was worried about putting all my proverbial career eggs in one basket, and I missed having a big team around every day. *But,* I thought, *if not now, then when?* Would there ever be a moment to fully invest in my dreams? Could I build a business around an active decision to work exclusively on projects that I feel passionate about with food companies that are genuinely seeking to change the world and people's lives, for the better, one delicious bite at a time? Another unknown—another risk—yet another "try?" *You betcha.*

So, I made the pivot. And let me tell you, *it has been the privilege of my life.* The companies growing up in the food world right now are truly amazing, with game-changing models around access to delicious, fresh, and affordable "good for you" menu options that walk the talk of putting people first. Everything I wanted, every value I strive to practice, all being put into action by smart, creative, and ambitious people, and I get to be a part of it. *The privilege of living this opportunity is real.* All because I stuck it out, held to my vision of impactful leadership, and never knowingly threw away a lesson from any of the experiences I had—good or bad.

In this season of raising a small child and running and growing a business, my commitment to the food world has only been emboldened. Consulting, coaching, and writing all feed my entrepreneurial spirit as well as my heart, which I know makes me a better mother, wife, friend, professional, and human. If I could wave a magic spatula and determine how my career will end, I know that I would actively choose to work until the end of my days. Because it's not really work to me—it's what I love, and how I love, and, ultimately, it's where home is. *You will have to pry work—and food—out of my cold, dead hands.* I also recognize so deeply what an honor it is to be able to share my personal learnings from all the years spent in the industry so far. My greatest hope is to inspire someone else's career journey for the better, to encourage them to be bold, take risks, say yes to opportunities, and, above all else, keep their own dreams and ambitions unapologetically front and center.

So, I want to ask you this once again, here and now: How do *you* want to spend your time in the days and years ahead? What do you want to accomplish in your life? What does success ultimately mean to you?

Food is so much more than sustenance, so much more than a necessity to exist. Food is bounty—in our bellies and especially in our lives. Food is pleasure, joy, connection, and all the things we love about life. Food is where everyone is welcome. Food is where you can make your dreams happen, laugh until your belly hurts, make your home, and change the world. But only if you *stay in it.*

Your individual impact on the world and all the personal ways you will imprint on other people's journeys through this industry by virtue of *your* leadership and service will be some of the greatest privileges of your lifetime. They certainly have been in mine, and I will always be eternally grateful for the surprising and awesome wild and precious ride. I hope that you, too, will be inspired to take up this challenge and accept this bountiful and delicious gift of opportunity.

I am behind you, beside you, and rooting for you—always.

GRATITUDE

THE WORDS "THANK YOU" don't even begin to cover the enormous gratitude I have for those of you who have made this book possible. I will start with Jennie Nash, the best book coach in the world. If you have a burning desire to write a book, get thyself to the best book coach in the biz. Jennie Nash. Thank you, Jennie, for believing in this project and in me. This book simply would not exist without you.

To the early supporters of this book (some of whom graciously tolerated some very rough drafts): Sam Polk, Erik Fyrwald, Michiel Bakker, Gigi-Anne Hoh, Larry Yee, Catherine Lederer, Irfan Dama, Ryan Cox, Eliza Norris, Jill Overdorf, Sebastian Wright, Sylvia Banderas Coffinet, Marie Chalita, Joelle Delbourgo, Lianne Scott, Tamara Monosoff, and Rajesh Setty. Thank you for lending your impeccable counsel and for giving me the priceless gift of your support and encouragement. I will never be able to cook you enough dinners to reward each of you for what you have given to me so generously, so please consider this an open and always standing invitation. There will forever be a place for you at my table.

To the incredible industry leaders and experts who so unreservedly and bigheartedly gave their time, insight, and personal stories for the Insider Dish videos: Gigi-Anne Hoh, Sheilina Henry, Dana Gunders, Bryce Fluellen, Casey Gleason, Maisie Ganzler, Sarah Nelson, Ashmeet Kaur, Zachary Thomas, Gilbert Verdugo, Juliana Stone, Brian Schwartz, Catherine Lederer, Michiel Bakker, and Stacey Payne. Thank you for your courageous voices at this table and for recognizing the power of standing together—as one industry—in order to swing the door open for the next generation of leaders. Your willingness to share things about your own, unique experiences—especially those that weren't perfect but are no less valuable—made this work so much more meaningful. You are *my* heroes and I admire you fiercely. *Thank you, friends.*

To the most amazing, talented, visual storytellers I have ever known: Ryan Cox, Andrew Cox, and Nelson Alley Media. Thank you for bringing these incredible career stories to life in such a beautiful and meaningful way.

To the Food Commons Leadership, Larry Yee and Jim Cochran. Thank you for inspiring me in ways I never could have anticipated. Your vision still keeps my brain awake and buzzing with ideas and inspiration all night. To Larry Keeley and the incredible team of designers and industry colleagues from that one fateful workshop in San Francisco so many years ago. Thank you for sharing your deep wisdom and experience. To the Los Angeles Food Policy Council. I am forever in debt to all of you for sharing so much of your experience generously over the years. Your imprint is one of the most precious of my life, and your collective work encourages me every single day.

To Michiel Bakker. Your leadership impacted and inspired me in ways I will never be able to fully articulate. My sincerest gratitude for sharing so much of your incredible wisdom and experience over the years, and especially for sharing it here.

To the utterly phenomenal Page Two publishing team: Jesse Finkelstein, Melissa Edwards (aka the most patient, skilled, and extraordinary editor on the planet), Steph VanderMeulen, Adrineh Der-Boghossian, Meghan O'Neill, Melissa Kawaguchi, and Taysia Louie. Thank you for partnering with me in imagining what this book could be, for sparking new innovation around old ways of learning, for your willingness to push boundaries and attempt things never attempted before, and then for bringing it all to life so masterfully. I am truly grateful for all of you. *Dream publishing team!*

To the amazing leaders, advisors, and champions I have had the good fortune to work with and learn from over the years: Fedele Bauccio, Matt Delaney, Alain Coumont, Philippe Le Roux, Clare Sheppard, Matt

Galo, Linda Joy Kattwinkel, Helene Kennan, Dr. Robert Siew, Sebastian Wright, Dr. Babak Tashakkor, Gagan Biyani, and Robert Barrett. Thank you for all the ways you have each individually impacted my life and my work, and for all you have shared, provoked, and inspired along the way.

To Sutha Balendran, Logan Boyle, and Viviane Assis. This book exists because of your amazing love for our daughter and the endless support you have given our family so generously over these past years. Thank you from the bottom of this mama's heart. I couldn't have done this without you.

To my Mama Angels: Mary Linam, Diane Cox, and Dr. Debra Felgen-Langer. Thank you for your tireless support over the decades, for never being afraid to kick my ass when I needed it, and for making me a better human and professional. May everyone experience the true gift of such a team of truth-telling, ass-kicking angels behind them.

In loving memory of David Weinberg, and to his daughter Mali. May you always know what an incredible human your dad was and how his fierce and unwavering support of this broken, troubled teen influenced my life journey and career beyond anything I could have ever hoped for.

To my childhood knock-off Easy-Bake Oven that cooked *absolutely nothing* and made me so stinkin' mad, and which set me up for a lifetime of "stubbornly figuring things out"; to my dearest Emilie-loo, my mom, JP, and James, and, most especially, to my beloved Harro and Frankie, without whom none of this would have ever been possible.

The only way to end this most important thank you note of my life is to thank every single person I have ever worked with and served over all the years. Especially my PBOD and all the incredibly hard-working and talented folks I have had the privilege to work alongside. You all marked me in different ways, and I am so very grateful for the experiences you gave me and the lessons learned. Yes, even the hard, shitty ones. *Especially those.* It has been a true honor to learn from all of you.

Thank you, precious food world, for the gift of opportunity that you have been, and always are, in all of our lives.

NOTES

1: What's On the Menu

When they decided to open a restaurant: "Sweetgreen Founders Reflect on Success, McDonough School of Business, Georgetown University, n.d., msb.georgetown.edu/news-story/sweetgreen-founders-reflect-on-success.

After not much more than a decade: Katie Roof and Crystal Tse, "Salad Chain Sweetgreen Attains $6 Billion Value in Debut," Bloomberg, November 18, 2021, bloomberg.com/news/articles/2021-11-18/salad-chain-sweetgreen-doubles-valuation-in-trading-debut.

But through his deeply personal journey: Sam Polk, "For the Love of Money," *New York Times*, January 19, 2014, nytimes.com/2014/01/19/opinion/sunday/for-the-love-of-money.html.

Everytable has also taken the learnings: Nicholas Upton, "Everytable Kicks Off 'Social Equity' Franchise Program, *Franchise Times*, January 15, 2021, franchisetimes.com/franchise_news/everytable-kicks-off-social-equity-franchise-program/article_b893319a-5762-11eb-8686-439330cf4496.html.

I went from being in charge: Avery Hartmans, "21 Photos of the Most Impressive Free Food at Google," *Business Insider*, August 26, 2016, businessinsider.com/photos-of-googles-free-food-2016-8.

And if you don't have a degree, then: Robert E. Scott and David Cooper, "Almost Two-Thirds of People in the Labor Force Do Not Have a College Degree," Economic Policy Institute, March 30, 2016, epi.org/publication/almost-two-thirds-of-people-in-the-labor-force-do-not-have-a-college-degree; see also Reid Wilson, "Census: More Americans Have College Degrees than Ever Before," The Hill, April 3, 2017, thehill.com/homenews/state-watch/326995-census-more-americans-have-college-degrees-than-ever-before.

. . . there are more women and minority managers: "Restaurant Industry Facts at a Glance, National Restaurant Association, National Statistics, restaurant.org/research-and-media/research/industry-statistics/national-statistics.

. . . and nine in ten restaurant managers: "National Restaurant Association Releases 2020 State of the Restaurant Industry Report," National Restaurant Association, February 27, 2020, restaurant.org/research-and-media/media/press-releases/national-restaurant-association-releases-2020-state-of-the-restaurant-industry-report.

2: Yes, You Have to Eat Your Lima Beans Before Dessert

But if you're feeling doubtful: See also Tomas Chamorro-Premuzic and Derek Lusk, "The Dark Side of Resilience," *Harvard Business Review*, August 16, 2017, hbr.org/2017/08/the-dark-side-of-resilience.

That's the story of Lara Merriken: "LÄRABAR: Lara Merriken," NPR, How I Built This, with Guy Raz, October 28, 2019, audio file, 56:00, npr.org/2019/10/18/771282092/l-rabar-lara-merriken; see also "Our Story," LÄRABAR, larabar.co.uk/our-story.

I know this because that's the story: Olivia Singh, "Brad Pitt Has 'No Shame' About His Job as an El Pollo Loco Mascot Before Making It Big in Hollywood: 'Man's Gotta Eat,'" Insider, September 13, 2019, insider.com/brad-pitt-el-pollo-loco-mascot-ellen-show-video-2019-9.

3: The Next Job After Your First Job

What we don't often discuss is that "career" is a verb, too: These definitions of "career" were taken from the Cambridge English Dictionary and the Oxford Languages dictionary for Google, respectively: dictionary.cambridge.org/us/dictionary/english/careered; google.com/search?q=career+definition.

I was stunned by the bizarre things: Nitamani Choudhury, Murlindhar Meghwal, and Kaylan Das, "Microencapsulation: An Overview on Concepts, Methods, Properties and Applications in Foods," Food Frontiers, Wiley Online Library, June 18, 2021, doi.org/10.1002/fft2.94.

4: From Mise to Plate

Back when I was working at Pret A Manger: Simon Neville, "Pret A Manger Staff Give Free Coffee to Their Favourite Customers, Sandwich Chain Boss Reveals," *London Evening Standard*, April 21, 2015, standard.co.uk/news/london/pret-a-manger-staff-give-free-coffee-to-their-favourite-customers-sandwich-chain-boss-reveals-10191611.html.

5: Fire, Knives, and Foolery

And while that famous "idiot sandwich" scene: "Hell's Cafeteria: Gordon Ramsay Grills Julie Chen & James," *The Late Show with James Cordon*, April 28, 2015, YouTube video, 1:39, youtube.com/watch?v=nqY3tv-y62A.

6: Happiness Is a Main Course, Not a Side Dish

Turns out, food was not: Todd Davis, "What President Barack Obama Learned in His First Job at Baskin-Robbins," *Dallas Morning News*, February 25, 2016, dallasnews.com/business/2016/02/25/what-president-barack-obama-learned-in-his-first-job-at-baskin-robbins.

9: The Real Bread and Butter

To give you a little more perspective: "McDonald's Reports Fourth Quarter and Full Year 2021 Results," McDonald's, January 27, 2022, corporate. mcdonalds.com/corpmcd/en-us/our-stories/article/press-releases.Q4-2021-results.html.

Their global systemwide sales reached: "McDonald's Reports Fourth Quarter."

To be clear, I'm not trying to pick on McDonald's: Julie Creswell, "McDonald's, Now with Higher Prices, Topped $23 Billion in Revenue in 2021," *New York Times*, January 27, 2022, nytimes.com/2022/01/27/business/mcdonalds-earnings.html

Do you think that seventeen-year-old Ingvar Kamprad: Callum Hoare, "IKEA: Incredible Meatballs Sales Exposed as Retailer Threatens Fast-Food Industry," *Express*, June 3, 2020, express.co.uk/life-style/life/1290791/ikea-meatball-delivery-fast-food-furniture-opening-restaurant-sales-sweden-coronavirus-spt.

11: Let's Break Bread and Change the World

Today, IKEA has leveraged its massive influence: "Highlights from the IKEA Sustainability Report FY21," About IKEA, Sustainability, about.ikea. com/en/sustainability/sustainability-report-highlights; "IKEA restaurant meals: 50% plant-based by 2025," November 23, 2020, About IKEA, Newsroom, about.ikea.com/en/newsroom/2020/11/23/ikea-restaurant-meals-50-plantbased-by-2025; Jessica Cherner, "How IKEA is (Nearly) Ending Plastic Packaging by 2025," *Architectural Digest*, December 7, 2021, architecturaldigest.com/story/ikea-eliminate-plastic-packagin; *Planet and People Positive: IKEA Group Sustainability Strategy for 2020*, IKEA, n.d., ikea-sustainability-strategy-people-planet-positive-2020-511938_v3.pdf.

…approximately 96 percent of undocumented Mexican workers: Examining the Economic Contributions of Undocumented Immigrants by Country of Origin, New American Economy Research Fund, report, March 8, 2021, research .newamericaneconomy.org/report/contributions-of-undocumented-immigrants-by-country.

According to the US Environmental Protection Agency: See Laura Sullivan, "How Big Oil Misled The Public Into Believing Plastic Would Be Recycled," NPR, September 11, 2020, npr.org/2020/09/11/897692090/

how-big-oil-misled-the-public-into-believing-plastic-would-be-recycled; see also United States Environmental Protection Agency, "Plastics: Material-Specific Data," Facts and Figures About Materials, Waste and Recycling, EPA, epa.gov/facts-and-figures-about-materials-waste-and-recycling/plastics-material-specific-data.

Now and for the past six decades: The Pew Charitable Trusts, "Fixing the Oversight of Chemicals Added to Our Food: Findings and Recommendations of Pew's Assessment of the U.S. Food Additives Program," November 7, 2013, pewtrusts.org/en/research-and-analysis/reports/2013/11/07/fixing-the-oversight-of-chemicals-added-to-our-food; see also US Food and Drug Administration, "CFR Code of Federal Regulations Title 21, accessdata.fda.gov/scripts/cdrh/cfdocs/cfcfr/cfrsearch.cfm?fr=101.22; Ashly Perez, "8 Foods We Eat In the U.S. That Are Banned In Other Countries," BuzzFeed, June 19, 2013, buzzfeed.com/ashleyperez/8-foods-we-eat-in-the-us-that-are-banned-in-other-countries; Tom Neltner and Maricel Maffini, *Generally Recognized as Secret: Chemicals Added to Food in the United States*, NRDC Report, Natural Resources Defense Council, April 2014, nrdc.org/sites/default/files/safety-loophole-for-chemicals-in-food-report.pdf.

While seat belts have been available: Dave Roos, "When New Seat Belt Laws Drew Fire as a Violation of Personal Freedom," History, August 31, 2020, history.com/news/seat-belt-laws-resistance.

12: From Management to Executive Leadership

There was one entry-level cook: "Clean and Cool Fruit Pops for Hot Summer Days," Food & Home, Goop, goop.com/food/recipes/detox-friendly-summer-popsicles.

Chef David Chang obviously recognized her talent: Maria Aspan, "How Milk Bar's Christina Tosi Went From Momofuku Employee to Bakery Chain CEO," Inc., n.d., inc.com/magazine/201804/maria-aspan/christina-tosi-milk-bar-momofuku-bakery.html.

Today, Chef Tosi has opened a bunch of Milk Bar locations: See Milk Bar's About page, milkbarstore.com/pages/about.

But while Chang lifted Tosi up: Hannah Selinger, "Life Was Not a Peach," Eater, December 21, 2020, eater.com/22193151/momofuku-david-chang-memoir-eat-a-peach-review.

THE OFFICIAL
TASTE OF OPPORTUNITY
COMPANION RECIPE EBOOK

IF YOU'VE TRIED A FEW of the recipes in this book and want even more flavors to accompany you on your delicious career journey, don't forget to download the companion recipe ebook, *The Complete "My Editor Wouldn't Let Me Put Them All in the Book" Companion to* A Taste of Opportunity: *A Few Favorite Recipes from My Unexpected, Unpredictable, Challenging, Wonderful, and Always Delicious Career in Food*! This is an easy reference for all twelve of the dishes you found in these pages, plus almost thirty more that I mentioned along the way but that my editor (whom we'll call "the Page Count Police") wouldn't let me include. Here's just a sample of what you'll find:

The promised "Storytelling" **Lasagne**

"Suffocating My Creativity & Your Profits"
Chilled Smoked Salmon Soup

"I Worked in European Kitchens and Endured SO MUCH
Garbage So You Don't Have To" **Perfect Crepe Batter**

"Perfectly Balanced Big Five" **Butter-Poached Lobster**

"Not Harry Hamlin's Incredible Bolognese,
BUT a Very Close Second" **Master Bolognese Sauce**

Go to **atasteofopportunity.com**, download, and start cooking!

ABOUT THE AUTHOR

RENEE GUILBAULT is a veteran food-industry consultant with expertise in large-scale, global, multi-unit food and beverage operations. Before launching her consulting firm, Essayer Food Consulting, Renee was instrumental in developing and executing operational, high-volume strategies and developing revolutionary food programming at Pret A Manger, Bon Appétit Management Company at Google, Compass Group, and Le Pain Quotidien.

Along the way, Renee ran a catering business, was a private chef and an executive chef, acted as a food ingredient broker, had a side gig cooking at the American Embassy Residence of the OECD ambassador in Paris, was fired as a server, became head of food for a food-tech start-up, and cooked for the Royal Automobile Club in London. Renee also held a role on the Los Angeles Food Policy Council Leadership Board and its coordinating committee for five years in support of her commitment to a more just and sustainable food system for all, and has worked as a board advisor to both regional food system projects and private sector efforts.

Today, Renee lives in Boston with her family, although *home* is always Pasadena, California, where the avocados and citrus grow freely and sunshine is on the menu most days of the year.

More Resources

Your prep for taking the food world by storm:

These career and leadership insights are truly the Chef's Kiss!

Where to Go From Here?

I mean, this can't be goodbye. It's just the beginning!

First of all, come say hi on Twitter **@GuilbaultRenee**. I'd love to hear from you! You can also find me and the kick-ass Mise Mode™ team at **essayerfoodconsulting.com** along with all sorts of awesome tools, tips, and insights.

Until next time, don't forget:
- Winging it is the norm.
- Imperfection is where the magic happens.
- You've got this!

CPSIA information can be obtained
at www.ICGtesting.com
Printed in the USA
BVHW090919030123
655384BV00017B/205